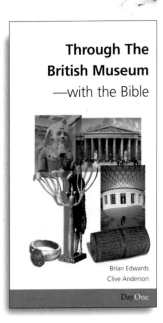

Through The British Museum

—with the Bible

Brian Edwards
Clive Anderson

Day One

Series Editor: Brian H Edwards

Day One

Through The
British Museum
—with the Bible

❸ Return to Egypt

An exotic land full of mummies, myths and monuments, beloved by authors and film makers because of Pyramids, romance, adventure and fabulous discoveries. Marvel at the skill of the craftsman and learn something of this ancient culture.

Rooms 65—Egypt

Black land—Red land

"Egypt is the gift of the Nile" according to the ancient Greek historian Herodotus. Egypt owed to the Nile its society, prosperity, religion and even its calendar—the three seasons of the Egyptian year were governed by the flow of the river. One of the earliest civilizations known to man, the ancient Egyptians called their land by two names: kemet (black land), referring to the black mud left by the receding flood waters in which crops could be grown, and deshret (red land), because in certain light the desert appears to glow red as a warning to any traveller.

An Egyptian priest and historian called Manetho in the third century BC wrote a history of Egypt called Aegyptica and he is credited with dividing Egyptian history into dynasties. His writings have not survived intact.

Above: A temple at Thebes built by Tuthmosis III showing a Christian icon painted on the second column (see below.)

Facing page: Ramesses II, thought by some to be the Pharaoh of the Exodus.

❷ Father Abraham

Five thousand years ago, southern Iraq, with its sophisticated society and impressive buildings, was a vibrant centre of trade. From here came a man whom Jews, Christians and Muslims all revere. Leaving Ur and a comfortable way of life he travelled as a nomad. See something of the rich culture of the country that he left.

You begin your tour from the Great Court. Tracing you are two staircases you can each side of the Reading Room. Take either side, and on the bridge at the top and enter Room 56—Early Mesopotamia

The world of Abraham—Early Mesopotamia

The word Mesopotamia means "between the two rivers" and it refers to the land between the great rivers Tigris and Euphrates in what is now southern Syria and down through Iraq to the Persian Gulf. This was the land of Israel's roots because from here, around 2000 BC, Abraham migrated family north to Haran and then south into the land of Canaan. In the next three rooms we will discover much that illustrates narratives in the book of Genesis and beyond; some of the names may be familiar to us.

Digging up Ur

The first serious archaeological excavations of Ur (now Tell el Muqayyar) in southern Iraq began in 1923 under the direction of

Above: Room 56—Early Mesopotamia—the world of Abraham

Facing page: The exquisite 'Ram caught in a thicket' from Ur of the Chaldees about 2600BC (Wh:122205). One of a pair found in the Great Death Pit. (Height: 45cm)

CONTENTS

© Day One Publications 2004 First printed 2004

All Scripture quotations are taken from the New International Version

A Catalogue record is held at The British Library   ISBN 1 903087 54.6

Published by Day One Publications PO Box 66 Leominster HR6 OXB

☎ 01568 613 740 email—sales@dayone.co.uk www.dayone.co.uk All rights reserved

Design and Art Direction: Steve Devane   Printed by CPD

Through the British Museum—footprints of the Bible

The British Museum is one of the finest museums in the world and home to seven million objects, with around seventy thousand of them on display in one hundred galleries.

The Museum was first opened in 1759 and at first it was accessible for just three hours a day for those who applied in writing, stating why they wished to visit. Today you can spend all day here without appointment and at no charge. There are guided tours or you can simply browse on your own. Some five million visitors take up this invitation each year—it is the second most popular tourist attraction in Britain after the Blackpool Pleasure Complex.

There are exhibits from every continent and covering the whole of the history of civilization. You can enjoy one of Europe's finest collections of Japanese art, or study the three-quarters of a million coins from the time of Daniel to the present day. You may wander around the mummies of Egypt or examine the beautiful sculpture of Ancient Greece. You can delve into the history of Africa and the Americas, or research the story of the Romans and Anglo Saxons in Britain.

But in this guide we have one object in mind. Instead of drifting around the Museum wondering what everyone else is so interested in, we will focus on those items that will help us in our understanding of the Bible and our early Christian heritage. Some will point to the accuracy of the Bible records whilst others will simply throw light on Bible stories and customs. We have also taken you into the intriguing world of Britain before the Romans left.

So, in a fascinating walk through Bible times, we will travel from the time of Abraham right up to the time of Paul, and take in the great empires of Egypt, Assyria, Babylon, Persia, Greece and Rome. We will wander through these powerful kingdoms —and end up in Britain!

Left: The magnificent Great Court, with over three thousand panes of glass

Welcome to the British Museum

Some useful information about the Museum

TRAVEL AND MUSEUM DIRECTIONS

The British Museum
Great Russell Street
London WC1 3DG
☎ +44(0) 20 7323 8000
www.thebritishmuseum.
ac.uk

MUSEUM HOURS OF OPENING

Saturday—Wednesday
10.00–17.30
Thursday—Friday
10.00–20.30
  Late viewing for many galleries is available on Thursdays and Fridays until 20.30.

GREAT COURT HOURS OF OPENING

Monday: 09.00–18.00
Tuesday—Wednesday:
09.00–21.00
Thursday—Saturday:
09.00–23.00
Sunday: 09.00–21.00
  Please note that Saturday is always a very busy day for the Museum.
  You are advised to check on the website for full details and any changes.

The best route to the Museum is to take the London Underground Northern Line to Tottenham Court Road. When you come out of this station there are a number of possible exits so look

Left: Tottenham Court Road Underground Station

for Exit 3 and the signs to the British Museum. From here it is a ten minute walk via Great Russell Street.

The Museum can also be reached from Holborn and Russell Square Underground stations but you will have a longer walk!

BUS ROUTES:

Tottenham Court Road, northbound, and Gower Street, southbound: 10, 24, 29, 73, & 134;
Southampton Row: 68, 91, & 188;
New Oxford Street: 7, 8, 19, 25, 38, 55, 55, 98, & 242.

ADMISSION CHARGE

There is **no admission charge,** though the Museum Trustees do request a donation of approximately £3 per person. Any currency is accepted. Alternatively you may

wish to consider becoming a **Friend of the British Museum,** the benefits of which include a quarterly magazine and a reduction on purchases in the museum shops.

The Museum website

The website address is: www.thebritishmuseum.ac.uk
The Museum provides an excellent facility for you to browse for specific items on the web. Simply go to: www.thebritishmuseum.ac.uk/compass. From **Compass** you can identify items, gather further information and even download pictures. Not all items in this guide will be found in Compass. When you are at the Museum, you can use Compass in the Reading Room (see note later). **Children's Compass**—a website designed especially for younger visitors: www.thebritishmuseum.

ac.uk/childrenscompass
School visits are welcome to the Museum.

General Information

A note of caution! It is never possible to guarantee that all the items referred to will be on display, or that all the rooms will be open. Some **exhibition rooms** may be closed for refurbishment or due to lack of staff, and some exhibits may be away on loan to other museums.

Above: The Museum shop in Great Russell Street

Refreshments in the Museum

The **Court café,** situated in the Great Court with two serving points, provides hot drinks and light refreshments. For something more substantial you can try the **Court Restaurant** just above the Great Court. If you take your lunch break outside the 'rush hour' of 1300 to 1400 hrs you will find a seat more easily!

If you bring a packed lunch and drink, these must be consumed outside in the Forecourt. You must not eat or drink in the galleries —and this includes chewing gum!

Above: *The cafe in The Great Court is a popular meeting place for Museum visitors*

You are well advised to telephone in advance if there is a particular exhibit or room that you wish to see. When you arrive, pick up a list of 'Gallery availability' from the **Information Desk** in the Great Court. This will give the times when certain rooms will be open; it will be easy to adjust your tour with the aid of this guide. If a room you wish to visit is not open at the stated time, ask at the information desk and they may arrange for an attendant to accompany you. Also, pick up a list of the 'Free Gallery Tours'—these change daily and you may wish to join one.

Please note also that whilst the details in this book are accurate at the time of publication, because the Museum is constantly being upgraded we cannot guarantee that any of the items are in the locations recorded here.

If you are not short of

Above: *The bookshop in The Great Court*

time, when you arrive stay a while to enjoy the magnificent Great Court. There is an excellent **book room** here plus a **souvenir shop** and **children's shop.** If you can afford something special, you should visit the **Grenville shop** with its array of replica jewellery, sculpture and silks.

Travel light around the museum, as there is a lot of walking. This guide is all that you really need unless you want a notebook and pencil for your own notes. You may also wish to have a small copy of the Bible with you. You can check any bags into the cloakroom for a small charge or keep a rucksack on your back, taking care that any valuables are not vulnerable to pickpockets.

The Museum is accessible for **disabled visitors,** and a limited supply of wheelchairs is available (phone to reserve on 020 7323 8299). Guide dogs are welcome in the Museum.

Toilet and baby changing facilities are available in the Great Court and toilets are also located in other areas of the museum.

You are allowed to take **photographs and**

52
Ancient Near East

videos, but you must not use a tripod. However, remember that a flash will normally flash-back from a glass case. If you are serious about photography use a high speed film without flash, or a high specification digital camera. Please note that you may use your pictures for personal use only; publication of your own pictures is forbidden.

You may use a **mobile phone** only in the Great Court area.

Please note that throughout the tour **you must not touch exhibits or lean on the glass display cases;** the eagle eye of the attendants will soon correct you if you do—or an alarm will sound! Visitors are advised that CCTV is in operation.

A **room number** refers to the room you are in—not the one you are about to enter.

Every item in the Museum has its own **accession number** and we have noted these for you so that you can be sure you are looking at the correct exhibit. The initial letters will indicate the gallery represented: for example EA refers to Egyptian Antiquity, ANE to Ancient Near East (formerly WA, Western Asiatic), and GR to Greece and Rome.

The **case numbers,** which we use to guide you to an object, are often indistinct—generally in white at the top left corner.

The story of the British Museum

The British Museum Act of 1753 authorised the building of 'one general repository' to house the collections of Sir Hans Sloane, the Harley and Cotton families, 'and of the additions thereto'. The British Museum as we know it today is made up largely of those 'additions thereto'. Montagu House in Bloomsbury was purchased, renovated and six years later—on 15 January 1759—a museum was opened. During the eighteenth century the collection built up with books and hardware brought here from around the world. The defeat of Napoleon in Egypt saw the Rosetta Stone (see page 78) added to the museum in 1802 and five years later Lord Elgin sold to the state the marble sculptures from the Parthenon and Erechtheum in Greece—the Elgin

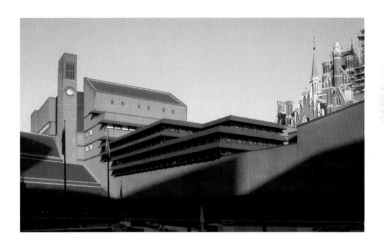

Above: The British Library, situated between Euston and St Pancras Stations, has possibly the finest collection of Bibles in the world among its 150 million items of literature

Facing page: The main entrance of the British Museum

Marbles (see page 100). During the nineteenth century, books, manuscripts, pottery, statues, coins, medals, botanical and zoological specimens, poured into the collection from statesmen and explorers, from both private and company collections. Soon the building was inadequate to house the fascinating collection and in 1823 an extensive rebuilding programme began. The façade that you see today with its fine Corinthian columns was completed in 1842, and the central Reading Room in 1857.

Expansion
But still the Museum grew. By 1881 the natural history collection had to be moved to South Kensington (now the Natural History Museum) but The Copyright Act of 1911, which required that a copy of every book published in Britain must be deposited with the Museum, further squeezed space. In 1973 the books and manuscripts came under the control of the British Library which in 1998 moved out of the British Museum into its impressive, purpose-built suite at St Pancras. This move included the magnificent display of Bibles and biblical manuscripts that were once housed in the Museum's King's Library.

The British Museum is a Grade I listed building. The Museum is owned by the nation and is governed by a Board of Trustees which is responsible to the British Parliament. The first popular guide to the Museum was published in 1808.

How long will this tour take?

The short answer is: 'As long as you have got!' To cover the whole of this guide in detail will take you more than a day. But don't let that discourage you, we can help you to fit the tour into whatever time you have available. Here are four ways of using this guide:

1. If you have a **full day** ahead of you, arrive early and follow this guide closely. Resist the temptation to wander off and look at other items—there is always so much to attract and distract your attention in the British Museum; make a note of areas you would like to return to on another occasion. If you stay with the guide and keep moving, you can complete it within the day—allowing a break for lunch.

2. If you are **short of time**, you will find an index on page 126 of some of the most significant items of the tour.

3. If you can arrange **return visits** on later occasions, this guide will make it very easy for you. Each chapter can be taken as a guide on its own so that you can cover a chapter or more on one visit and then continue on subsequent occasions. If you have a particular interest and limited time then you can start with the chapter of your choice.

4. Perhaps you are just an **armchair enthusiast** who is not able to visit the museum. This guide will enrich your understanding of the Bible. It is also a valuable research tool for all who preach and teach the Bible.

A number of technical words will be encountered in our tour: they are all explained in 'A glossary of

Left: The roadside gateway to the British Library on Euston Road

Left: Tuthmosis III, with Ramesses II in the background. One of these is probably the Pharoah of the Exodus. The straight beard of Ramesses (as opposed to it being curled at the end) indicates that the statue was carved during his lifetime

archaeological words' on page 120.

In the tour presented in this guide there is an overall chronological order, but we have tried to avoid constant 'back-tracking'. In order to achieve this, some items appear out of sequence. We will make it clear when this happens.

Instructions for your route are in blue and therefore are easy to distinguish from the descriptive text.

Two excellent companion books to fill out the details of this travel guide are:

The Bible in the British Museum—interpreting the evidence by TC Mitchell, The British Museum Press (ISBN 0 7141 1698). This is available in the Museum Bookshop.

Discoveries from Bible Times by Alan Millard, Lion Publishing 1997 ISBN 0 7324 1608 6.

Some of the dimensions of the exhibits given in the text are approximate.

We have used the *New International Version* translation of the Bible as its spelling of names closely reflects those used in the Museum. Because of continuous study and discoveries, scholars may alter names (and spelling) for kings and peoples from the ancient world; for the sake of clarity this guide generally uses those in current use on the Museum's identification labels.

1 Before you begin

Household waste and the spoils of war, along with apparently unexciting trash, are an archaeologist's dream. Alongside monuments, inscriptions and statues, these commonplace items help to bring the past to life. They are also a boon to the travel industry, as thousands of tourists flock to visit the lands where all yesterday's leftovers have been found

Archaeology is rubbish!

Above: With touch-screen digital technology, the Reading Room is open to Museum visitors

Facing page: The British Museum Reading Room was completed in 1857 and has been used by many famous people since then

Archaeology is the science of reading history from the leftovers of previous civilizations. It involves uncovering the remains of buildings and of household bits and pieces. From these we learn who the people were and when and how they lived. Archaeology has been called 'the study of durable rubbish.'

It is an exciting science because we are looking through a window into the past and watching a way of life that would otherwise be wholly unknown to us. A burnt and broken wall may speak of a long lost civilization that came to a violent end; a piece of shattered pottery with a hurried note scrawled on it informs us of a disastrous military campaign; a beautiful vase clearly foreign to the location in which it was found tells us of international trade; a hastily buried cache of coins and household valuables points to the disintegration of a community. The past is right there in front of us.

Above: *The tomb of Cyrus at Pasargadae. When Alexander the Great visited it he discovered the tomb had been raided by grave robbers*

The word archaeology comes from the Greek *archaios* which means 'ancient' or 'old' and *hoi archaiois* meant 'the men of old'. The Greeks used the word *archaiologia* to refer to a traditional story or legend. Bishop Hall of Norwich first used it in English in 1607 to refer to the Bible narratives. Not until the early nineteenth century did the word 'archaeology' come to be used of items that could be dug out of the ground. Today the same word can cover anything discovered from the past, including manuscripts.

Grave events

The earliest 'archaeologists' were grave robbers who plundered ancient royal tombs for their treasures. In the year 529 BC, Cyrus II—the great Persian King whom we will meet later in our tour—died whilst on a military campaign. Inscribed above his magnificent tomb was the command: 'O man, whoever you are and whenever you come, for I know that you will come—I am Cyrus, who gave the Persians their empire. Do not grudge me this patch of earth that covers my body.' However, when Alexander the Great climbed the steps to inspect it in 322 BC, he discovered that the robes, cape, jewellery and scimitar of Cyrus were gone, and his bones lay all over the floor of the stone coffin. Modern scientific archaeologists are far more respectful and careful in their work.

Empires, archaeologists—and the Bible

Archaeology is a fairly young science. Little serious archaeological work was done before the nineteenth century, but as western nations extended their empires and trade into territories little known before, a whole new world opened up. After the defeat of Napoleon, British and French archaeologists worked together in Egypt.

Present day Iraq has proved to be a treasure-trove for archaeologists. In 1843 Paul Botta, a French archaeologist, excavated at the city of Khorsabad, and the fabulous palace of Sargon II (Isaiah 20:1) came to light. Two years later a young Englishman, Austen Henry Layard, uncovered Nimrud (its ancient name was Calah or Kalhu, see Genesis 10:8–11). From 1847–51 he worked at the great city of Nineveh (Genesis 10:11), and discovered the palace of Sennacherib—including the now famous Lachish victory room (see pages 88–90). From 1835–1837, Major (later Sir) Henry Rawlinson and others deciphered the Assyrio-Babylonian language and worked on the cuneiform tablets discovered by Layard at Nimrud and Nineveh—particularly the rich library of Ashurbanipal. In 1875 George Smith published Babylonian stories of creation and a great flood.

For the first time, the Bible was being looked at in the context of what could be learnt about the nations surrounding Israel. Archaeological societies sprang into being and now 'Libraries were ransacked for hidden documents and the earth itself for the remnants of lost civilizations.' History in general and archaeology in particular was no longer the work of amateurs or treasure hunters; slowly it was developing into what it is today— an exact and exciting science.

Left: Fast food from Thebes: including duck, bread, fruit and fish. These were included in Egyptian tombs as food for the Ka— the surviving spirit of the departed. Thebes was the ancient city of Upper Egypt on the banks of the Nile. By 1600 BC it became the capital of all Egypt

Professor Alan Millard describes archaeology as 'a scientific exploration of the past'.

At first the cultures of the Ancient Near East or Mesopotamia—lands known today as Syria and Iraq—and of Egypt in North Africa were studied for their own sake, without any direct link with the Bible. However, soon the names of some of the rulers of these civilizations were found who could be identified with those mentioned in the Bible, and in these ancient records names of kings of Israel and Judah, as well as place names mentioned in the Bible, occasionally appeared. A new interest was aroused. At the same time, the discoveries of Sir William Ramsay—who spent his time exploring in Asia Minor (Turkey)—showed that the history written by Dr Luke in his Gospel and the Acts of the Apostles was accurate. Biblical archaeology had come to birth.

There are many instances where the Bible was once thought to be either in error or was simply inventing names, but new discoveries have confirmed the truth of the biblical record. One example of this is the reference in Isaiah 20:1 to King Sargon who we will meet later (see page 87). But this is not the main value of archaeology, because the trustworthiness of the Bible rests on different criteria. The chief significance of archaeology is that it throws light upon many of the narratives, and helps us to understand how people lived and what was happening in the world at that time. This is 'the ambience of history'. As you look at the exhibits you will gain a 'feel' for the atmosphere of life in Bible times.

Above: Relief from the Siege of Lachish—an event from the time of King Hezekiah of Judah in 701 BC (see pages 88–90)

Above: The tell of Beth Shan stands 80 metres high

What does a Tell tell us?

Ancient civilizations built their towns on the rubble—often with the rubble—of the previous occupants. All that the earlier people left behind—their building materials, pottery, jewellery, messages, food remains, household utensils, weapons and even their own bones—were covered over by the newcomers. It is all this 'durable rubbish' that helps the archaeologist. As generation after generation built upon the trash of their ancestors—or of the enemy they defeated—the town grew higher and higher. The great mountain of earth that betrays the presence of an old city is called a *tell*, an Arabic and Hebrew word for 'ruin-mound'. This word is found in the names of Bible cities like Tel-melah and Tel-harsha (Nehemiah 7:61) and Tel-abib (Ezekiel 3:15).

Beth Shan (Bethshean) provides a fine example of a tell. This strategic city guarded the crossings of the River Jordan. First excavated in the 1920s and 30s, it reveals a long history of continuous occupation from the 5th millennium BC to the 11th century AD. Egyptian Pharaohs imposed their rule here. The Amarna letters (page 44) refer to reinforcements being sent here; and Rameses II placed a Philistine mercenary garrison in the well fortified city. The bodies of King Saul and his sons were hung on the city walls after the Battle of Gilboa (1 Samuel 31:8–13). Remains of a temple have been discovered, and this may well be the temple of Dagon in which the head and armour of Saul and Jonathan were paraded by the Philistines (1 Chronicles 10:10). David and Solomon secured it as part of Israel (1 Kings 4:7,12) but the records of Shishak of Egypt claim it as part of his conquests; this was in the time of Rehoboam.

Dating exhibits

The events recorded in the Bible are each located at a particular time in history, and in order to understand exhibits in the museum it is helpful to try and place them in their historical framework. This is their 'chronological context'. The word *chronology* comes from the Greek word for time—*chronos*.

In the Bible, events are often dated precisely, but the dating is never given with reference to the calendar as we know it. Sometimes a natural phenomenon is used as the marker, as in Amos 1:1. 'The words of Amos ... two years before the earthquake when Uzziah was king of Judah ...' or more often the reign of another king as in 2 Kings 13:1,10, and of course the census at the time of the birth of Jesus Christ in Luke 2:1, and the governorships of Felix and Festus in Acts 24:27. But this only helps us if we can locate those events or reigns at a point in history. In order to establish a chronology, the Bible's dates are compared with events in the surrounding nations; even so, exact dating is not always possible, and this is why the date for many exhibits is given as *circa* (or just *c.*), meaning 'about'.

Like any science, archaeology must be cautious and ready to change when new evidence is uncovered. An example of this is seen in the excavation of ancient Jericho. During the 1930s, Professor John Garstang from the University of Liverpool in England, excavated the old city of Jericho and discovered huge walls that had obviously been broken down, together with a city that had been plundered and set on fire; by pottery and other items he

Above: The recently restored ceiling of the Victorian Entrance Hall

Above: The stela of Ashurnasirpal II in the Great Court (ANE 118805). He ruled over the Assyrian empire during the reigns of Asa and Jehoshaphat in Judah. Above his hand are conventional symbols of his gods

dated the destruction of the city at around 1407 BC. This would fit a mid-fifteenth century date for the conquest of Canaan under Joshua. However, in 1958 Dame Kathleen Kenyon completed her own research into Jericho and redated Garstang's finds one thousand years earlier! She concluded that in Joshua's time there was no large city on the site. Then in 1978 John Bimson

published the results of his own research and argued in favour of Garstang's date. More recently Professor Kenneth Kitchen, an Egyptologist at the University of Liverpool, has argued against Bimson's dating. All this indicates the caution with which the results of archaeological dating should be received; there is a danger in drawing firm conclusions from little support. However archaeologists and historians can often arrive at precise dates through diligent work, especially when the ancient records refer, for example, to an eclipse of the sun or the appearance of a comet.

Commencing your tour

You will enter the Museum by the Victorian Entrance Hall.

This was opened in 1847 and the Polychrome scheme used motifs taken from buildings in ancient Athens. The Hall was damaged during World War II but the restoration that was completed in the year 2000 reinstated the hall to its original design. Some 65 different colours were discovered, and skilled craftsmen from English Heritage, using the latest scientific equipment and hand mixing natural pigments, have enabled us to enjoy the front hall and the main staircase just as generations of Victorians and Edwardians did. So, before you enter the Great Court with its outstanding contemporary architecture, take a moment to look up and around at this imitation of ancient Athens, a monument to Victorian art and an example of modern craftsmanship.

Left: The room of Egyptian sculpture (Room 4) is a significant attraction for the millions of visitors to the Museum. The exhibits here include the Rosetta Stone and the bust of Ramesses II

The Great Court

You now move into the magnificent Great Court (see picture on page 4), the size of a soccer pitch and the largest glass covered square in Europe with 3,312 panes of glass each uniquely cut to size. It was opened in the Millennium year and visitors gain the wonderful experience of feeling that they are in the open air whilst being warm and dry. Around the Great Court are sculptures that represent the various galleries. In the centre is the historic Reading Room and on either side are two impressive marble staircases that lead you to the upper floors. Alternatively lifts are available.

The Reading Room

Facing you as you enter the Great Court is the Museum's centre piece. The circular Reading Room is appropriately at the very heart of the Museum and we recommend that you look in and experience the atmosphere of this wonderful centre of study and information. You are seeing it just as it was when it was first opened in 1857, though the addition of computers has brought it into the

new millennium. Scores of prominent people have studied here, including Thomas Carlyle, Charles Dickens, Edward Elgar, Karl Marx and Oscar Wilde.

You may freely use one of the terminals to search for items in the Museum or gain additional information for many of the exhibits referred to in this guide. Simply go to the Home Page and click on Compass. It is so user-friendly that you do not need any knowledge of computers, but the staff will always help you if you ask. One excellent facility, especially if you are visiting from overseas, enables you to order a picture of an exhibit and collect it before you leave! However, not all exhibits are yet available on Compass. The Paul Hamlyn Library on the ground floor of the Reading Room is open to you as a reference library; there is a children's section of this library also.

You are now ready to begin your tour of the Bible in the British Museum.

Remember the Museum room plans are on the inside back cover.

A timeline from Abraham to Solomon

The dates for Hebrew kings can be established accurately by connecting them with kings and events of surrounding nations (especially Egypt, Assyria and Babylonia) whose dates are sometimes given by astronomical data. As a result of this, for example, the year of Ahab's death can be fixed as 853 BC, and this enables us to work both backwards and forwards from there using biblical data. This timeline assumes the accuracy of the ages and periods stated in the Old Testament.

BC	
2166	Abraham was born.
2091	Abraham left Haran at the age of 75 (Genesis 12:4).
2066	Isaac was born when Abraham was 100 (Genesis 21:5).
2006	Jacob was born when Isaac was 60 (Genesis 25:26).
1915	Joseph was born 17 years before entering Egypt which was 39 years before Jacob entered Egypt (Genesis 45:6 i.e. Joseph's age of 30 plus 7 years of plenty and 2 years of famine).
1898	Joseph was sold into Egyptian slavery at the age of 17 (Genesis 37:2).
1885	Joseph entered Pharaoh's service at the age of 30 (Genesis 41:46).
1876	Jacob settled in Egypt at the age of 130 (Genesis 47:9) and 430 years before the Exodus (Exodus 12:41).
1859	Jacob died at the age of 147 and 17 years after he settled in Egypt (Genesis 47:28).
1805	Joseph died at the age of 110 years (Genesis 50:26).
1526	Birth of Moses—he was around 80 at the time of the Exodus (Exodus 7:7).
1446	The Exodus: the Hebrews left Egypt 480 years before Solomon's fourth year (1 Kings 6:1)—see page 70 for a note on dating the Exodus, but this guide assumes a fifteenth century date.
1406	Death of Moses at the age of 120, and the beginning of the conquest of Canaan (Deuteronomy 34:7).
	Joshua took command in his early 60s (on the basis that the 'young man' of Exodus 33:11 would not be much more than 20; see Numbers 14:26–30).
1356	Joshua died at the age of 110 (Joshua 24:29).
1356–1050	Period of the Judges.
1050–1010	Saul's reign. Precise accuracy of these dates is not possible since Saul's exact age and length of reign in 1 Samuel 13:1 is not given.
1010–971	David's reign. He began at the age of 30 (2 Samuel 5:4) and therefore was born in 1040.
966	This year is accepted by scholars as the fourth of Solomon's reign. In this year he began to build the temple; this was 480 years after the Exodus (1 Kings 6:1). The Exodus itself was 430 years after Jacob settled in Egypt (Exodus 12:41).
970–930	Solomon's reign (2 Chronicles 9:30).

❷ Father Abraham

Five thousand years ago, southern Iraq, with its sophisticated society and impressive buildings, was a vibrant centre of trade. From here came a man whom Jews, Christians and Muslims all revere. Leaving Ur and a comfortable way of life he travelled as a nomad. See something of the rich culture of the country that he left

You begin your tour from the Great Court. Facing you are two staircases one on each side of the Reading Room. Take either side, cross the bridge at the top and enter **Room 56—Early Mesopotamia**

The world of Abraham—Early Mesopotamia

The word Mesopotamia means 'between the two rivers' and it refers to the land between the great rivers Tigris and Euphrates in what is now east Syria and down through Iraq to the Persian Gulf. This was the land of Israel's roots because from here, around 2000 BC, Abraham migrated firstly north to Haran and then south into the land of Canaan. In the next three rooms we will discover much that illustrates narratives in the book of Genesis and beyond; some of the names may be familiar to us.

56
Early
Mesopotamia

Digging up Ur

The first serious archaeological excavations of Ur (now Tell el Muqayyar in southern Iraq) began in 1923 under the direction of

Above: Room 56—Early Mesopotamia—the world of Abraham

Facing page: The exquisite 'Ram caught in a thicket' from Ur of the Chaldeans about 2600BC (WA121201). One of a pair found in the Great Death Pit. (Height: 40cm)

Above: *The remains of the ziggurat at the site of ancient Ur of the Chaldeans (now Tell al-Muqayyar), during the excavations by Sir Leonard Woolley in 1924, on behalf of the British Museum and the University Museum, Philadelphia. This is a building with which Abraham would have been familiar*

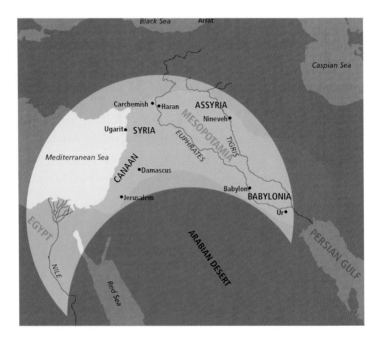

The Fertile Crescent—from Egypt to Mesopotamia to the Persian Gulf—in the time of Abraham

Above: Egyptian hieroglyphic writing

Sir Leonard Woolley. It is generally accepted that this is the site of the ancient 'Ur of the Chaldeans'—the birthplace of Abraham (Genesis 11:27–29). Although most of the artefacts in Room 56 are dated around 2500 BC—four hundred years prior to Abraham—they provide an accurate picture of the advanced civilization into which Abraham and Sarah were born. A huge ziggurat (temple) dedicated to the moon-god Nanna (also called Sin) dominated the skyline and lifestyle of the people of Ur. Such structures are reflected in the tower of Babel referred to in Genesis 11:1–9. Abraham may well have enjoyed the comfort of a two-storey brick house with a lobby, courtyard, kitchen and toilet, bedrooms and reception rooms; Sarah could have been accustomed to wearing beautifully intricate head-dresses and jewellery. Trade, literature, mathematics and astronomy were highly developed. Literacy was widespread—Sir Leonard Woolley discovered that one fifth of all homes in Ur contained clay tablets with writing.

Although it means by-passing some items that we will come back to in a moment, as you enter **Room 56**, turn left and cross to the opposite wall and *case 3*

This is an interesting display on the history of writing. A few

Above: Writing cuneiform on soft clay

A short history of writing

Writing is one of the important marks of civilization. The earliest known writing comes from Sumer (now southern Iraq) shortly before 3000 BC. Simple pictures (pictograms) were drawn in vertical columns on clay tablets with a pen made from a sharpened reed (See an example at the bottom right-hand corner of case 3).

In Egypt, writing appeared slightly later.

This hieroglyphic script of about 700 pictorial signs was written from left to right, right to left, or downwards! A cursive form, called 'hieratic' was developed in the Old Kingdom, and 'demotic' (meaning 'of the people') shorthand from about 700 BC.

Cuneiform 'wedge' script developed from the pictograms in Sumer. With about 300 signs, its use was confined to trained scribes, as was Egyptian. From about 2,000 BC cuneiform was the common script across the Fertile Crescent, but the alphabet, invented after 2,000 BC, began to replace it after 1,000 BC. With only 22 consonantal signs, its comparative simplicity meant more people could write and read it. Hebrew and Aramaic were written with the alphabet. As Aramaic became the official language under the Persian Empire in the 6th century BC, the alphabet was current from southern Egypt to the Indus River.

The conquest of Alexander the Great about 330 BC brought Greek to replace Aramaic, and so spread the Greek alphabet over the same area. Nevertheless, the Aramaic script survived and gave rise to both the modern Arabic and Hebrew alphabets.

The Egyptians invented papyrus (a form of paper made from the papyrus reed) and that, or leather (vellum was a high quality leather) , became the normal writing material wherever the alphabet was current. The 'paper and ink' referred to in 2 John 12 was almost certainly papyrus and the ink was made from soot mixed with gum.

Above: A reconstruction by A Forestier of the King's Grave

Below: The head dress of the royal lady from the Great Death Pit (WA 120834)

minutes here will prove valuable as an introduction to much of the form of writing that we will meet later. The information boards, **The origins of writing** and **The evolution of cuneiform writing** are worth reading. See Box: A short history of writing (facing page).

Cuneiform was impressed onto soft clay with a stylus and then baked or hardened in the sun; alternatively it was cut onto stone. The tablets were stored in baskets or on shelves, and are excellent for the archaeologist as they are virtually indestructible. The recorded history of this region begins with the first evidence of

writing about a thousand years before Abraham.

Start at the left of *case 3* where you find early writing in the form of pictures around 3000 BC.

On the move

Inventories and business documents on sun-dried clay bear witness to civilization and trade throughout the region. For a century Ur was the capital city of the area, but about 2000 BC tribes from the north-west overran Babylonia; they are known to history as the Amorites.

Genesis 11:31 reads, 'Terah took his son Abram… and his daughter-in-law Sarai [later called Sarah, see Genesis 17:15] and together they set out from Ur of the Chaldeans to go to Canaan. But when they came to Haran, they settled there.' Strictly, the name Chaldea would not be given to the land for another thousand years. With the destruction of Ur, the Amorites strengthened Babylon, a city that would later give its name both to the area and to an empire so feared by the Hebrew kings. Marduk became the national god of Babylon and his massive temple adorned the city (see later in Room 55 case 16 on page 54).

In *case 11* on the wall opposite *'The evolution of cuneiform writing'* are items from a temple close to the home of Abraham. Though 500 years before him, life changed only slowly in those days so they are still typical. As an illustration of the craftsmanship, notice the frieze of carved white stone on a bitumen background (WA116741–2) and the artificial flowers (WA1919–10–11 2591).

In the centre of the room here in *case 9* notice the musical instruments typical of Abraham's time. Later we will see one of these illustrated in the Standard of Ur. These instruments have been reconstructed from items found in the Royal Graves.

In *case 5* there are exquisitely carved decorations of shell and stone, some from Ur itself.

Now go to the back of *case 5* which is *case 13* **The King's Grave**

A poisoned Chalice
The King's Grave *case 13*

Between 1927 and 1932 Sir Leonard Woolley uncovered a cemetery in Ur. Sixteen of the tombs were dated around 2600 BC and were clearly the graves of royalty revealing much of the splendour of the courts at that time. All the items displayed in cases here come from the royal graves at Ur. In a grisly display of hope in the future life, courtiers, attendants, grooms and guards would assemble around the body

Above: The Royal Game of Ur (WA120834). Length: 28cm

Above: The standard of Ur—one of the earliest known illustrations of an army in battle formation (WA121201) Length: 48cm

of their master or mistress and then drink a poison in order to continue service in the next world—they were even accompanied by the oxen harnessed to their wagons. On display are items from the *King's Grave (case 13)*, the grave of **Queen Pu-Abi** *(cases 10 to your left, and 6 which is at the back of 10)*. The queen was buried beside the king—whose grave appears to have been partially robbed at the time of his wife's burial. Notice the beautiful jewellery that formed part of the dress of a royal lady.

Case 12 **The Great Death Pit** contains items from the grave of an unknown royal person. Here, the bodies of six guards were found together with the remains of sixty-four richly clothed attendant women. Small cups, presumably for the poison, lay beside each body. Notice the beautiful head-dress and jewellery. See picture on page 29.

Games and goats

Beyond the centre of the room, notice **The Royal Game of Ur** *(WA120834)* in *case 16*. This is a very old game (2,600 BC) and even Abraham might have played it. Unfortunately no one left us the rules, but you can buy a replica of it in the Museum shop. Later in our tour you will discover that guards outside the great city of Khorsabad idled away their time by playing this very game—1200 years later! See pages 91–92.

Further down in *case 28* there is the curious '*Ram caught in a thicket*' *(WA121201)* but resist the temptation to assume that it has anything to do with the story of Isaac in Genesis 22:1–13. See picture on page 24. Notice also the intricately carved **Standard of Ur**

A Babylonian story of the Flood— the Atrahasis Epic

This account comes from after the time of Abraham, around 1635 BC, although the story predates this. The account of creation has little in common with the version in Genesis. Anu is the god who rules in heaven, whilst Enlil rules the minor gods on the earth. When they down tools and refuse to work any more, man is created out of blood and clay. Unfortunately the noise from this rapidly increasing race gives Enlil a headache and so he deluges the earth with a Flood. Here the story converges a little more with the biblical account of Noah. Atrahasis is the hero of the Flood who, warned in advance, escapes in a boat with his family and the animals. When the Flood recedes, Atrahasis offers sacrifice to the gods. Compare the later Gilgamesh Epic in Room 55 case 10 (pages 55–56).

Above: A Babylonian story of the Flood (WA 78941)

(WA121201) which depicts peace on one side—note the lyre at the top right—and war on the other; this is one of the earliest known illustrations of an army in battle formation: light spearmen, charioteers, and elite guards flank the king. Both these items come from the royal tombs.

Case 25 (next to the ram in the thicket) *Babylonian Science and Literature* is a fascinating collection, which perfectly illustrates the society from which Abraham was called. Follow the exhibits through as they are described here.

Magic, myths and maths. The priests of Ur were busy with their elaborate duties at the gigantic ziggurat of the moon god, Sin. Under *Omens*, notice the clay model of a sheep's liver (WA92668). Marks on the livers of animals were used to aid the priests in their divination and this

Above: A clay model of a sheep's liver used in divination (WA92668)

one may have been used to teach trainees what to look for in each section—hence the holes. Ezekiel 21:21 records how King Nebuchadnezzar of Babylon 'will seek an omen (and) examine the liver' before deciding which city to attack. Close by are omens from a sheep's liver and stomach for divination *(WA17309 and WA96948)* and a record of magic spells *(WA96704 and WA109215)*.

The *Babylonian Story of the Flood (WA78941)*, known as the Atrahasis Epic is a Babylonian story of Creation and the Flood. See Box on opposite page.

Notice the large clay tablet of *geometrical calculations (WA15285)*. This and other tablets reveal that the Babylonians had a correct understanding of

astronomy, mathematics and geometry—including the theorem of Pythagoras nearly fifteen hundred years before the Greek philosopher wrote it down!

Singing from the same hymn sheet

On the second shelf down in *case 25* is a Babylonian hymn *(WA23584)* and an index giving the first lines! *(WA23701)*.

Education, education …
Education was as important then as now and here is a writing tablet on which the teacher wrote out the exercise on one side and the pupil copied it on the other *(WA104096)*. Clay tablets like these are of immense help to archaeologists deciphering ancient languages.

And now to war An early account of a military campaign (WA139965).

Just what the doctor ordered (on the third shelf) Here is an early prescription for drugs to cure a skin complaint. *(WA113970).*

Business as usual

To your left in *case 26* notice the small tablets of clay which was the 'paper' of Abraham's time. Baked hard in the sun, the completed document would last almost indefinitely. Thousands of these official records reveal a bustling city of merchants and businessmen trading across into Syria and down to the Persian Gulf. They record purchases (including complaints about wrong orders), marriages, and all the events of the life of a busy city. Notice that there is even a clay envelope to protect the clay letter (in the centre *WA113577*). Here also are agricultural implements from the time of Abraham.

Ancient ID cards

Cross over to *case 23* which contains a number of *cylinder seals* mounted on a panel to the right; they are dated from the time of Jacob and Judah. The Babylonians developed the cylinder seal and these are common throughout our tour of the Museum. They represent the Visa or ID card of the day. Rolled over soft clay the design became the owner's 'signature'. An

Clay letter   Inside of envelope   Top of envelope

Above: A Babylonian clay legal document with its envelope similar to WA113577. This one, in a private collection, is dated early 18th century BC and is a contract with 11 witnesses for the purchase of an office in the temple. Notice how the writing on the back of the cuneiform text becomes impressed on the inside of the envelope. Height of envelope: 11cm

Above: Cylinder seals were common in the ancient world and acted as the personal signature for a transaction. This seal of the 8th century BC depicts the goddess Ishtar standing on a lion (ANE 89769). The reversed bow is a sign of peace

interesting illustration of this is found in the sordid account of Judah consorting with what he thought was a prostitute but who was in reality his daughter-in-law, Tamar. When Judah was unable to pay her 'fee', she demanded as a pledge his staff and 'your seal and your cord' (Genesis 38:18). You will notice that each seal has a hole bored through the centre through which a cord could be threaded so that the seal could be hung safely around the owner's neck—or a pin inserted to fix to clothing. Jezebel used King Ahab's seal in order to secure the murder of Naboth (1 Kings 21:8).

In *case 22* you will find a reference to ***Hammurapi*** (sometimes spelt Hammurabi). He is not mentioned in the Bible, but was king of the Old Babylonian (Amorite) Dynasty from 1792–1750 BC, which places him somewhere between Abraham and Moses. His laws form one of the oldest known law lists in the world and some bear a resemblance to the Old Testament laws: for example his reference to dealing with the goring ox can be paralleled with Exodus 21:28–36. But the differences are equally significant and some of his punishments are excessive: anyone caught looting at a fire was to be thrown onto the fire and the doctor who failed to cure his patients was punished! Hammurapi's prologue extols the virtues, achievements and piety of the king, but there is no sacrifice offered for those who fail to keep the laws. The original black stone text is in the Museé du Louvre in Paris.

In *case 23* (bottom centre) you will find the genealogy of Hammurapi on a small clay tablet (WA80328); family lists like these help archaeologists to fix dates.

Genealogies (family trees) were very important in the ancient world; this is why we have the record of Abraham's ancestors in Genesis 11 and the long lists in Chronicles. The Levites in Nehemiah 7:61–65 who could not find their family records were excluded from the priestly service. The genealogies of Jesus in Matthew 1 and Luke 3 are significant in establishing his human ancestry.

In *case 24* (to the right) you will find a stone relief of Hammurapi (*WA22454*).

Snake bites and stone idols

In *case 19* (at the back of *case 22*) notice the *ritual trough* with the snake decoration coiling around it (*WA125929*). In the ancient world the snake represented both death (by its poisonous bite) and healing (by its ability to shed its skin). The concept would have been familiar to the Israelites when Moses placed a snake on a pole as a symbol of both death, as a result of their disobedience, and life if they trusted in God (see Numbers 21). This incident is used by Jesus to illustrate his coming death in John 3:14–18. The snake on a pole later developed into the apothecary's sign that is still used today.

In case 27 notice the *terracotta figurines and plaques*.

Above: A monument of Hammurapi (WA22454)

Above: A clay ritual trough. In the ancient world the snake represented both death and life (WA125929) Length: 30cm

No. 4 *(WA127497)* may be similar to the 'household gods' that Rachel would have taken from her father's home (Genesis 31:17–35), that Joshua complained of in Joshua 24:14–15, that Micah kept in his home (Judges 17–18), and that David's wife Michal owned (1 Samuel 19:13). These references reveal that for half a millennium some Israelites treasured household idols.

From the time of Abraham, it would be logical to cross into Room 63 and explore the time of Joseph in Egypt. However, many of the Egyptian exhibits are downstairs on the main floor, and to avoid having to return to where you are now, we will make a leap of time to the period of the kings of Israel and Judah.

From **Room 56** return back into **Room 57**.

Above: A terracotta plaque of the intercessor goddess Lamma (WA 127497). From Ur c.2000–1750BC during the time of the patriarchs Height: 40cm

❸ Who wants neighbours?

Israel found herself surrounded and constantly in battles and skirmishes with her immediate neighbours like the Philistines and Syrians. She was also the victim of the powerful empire-building war machine of the more distant Assyrians and Babylonians

This room provides a background to the turbulent days of the judges and kings of Israel. **The tour continues into Room 57 Ancient Near East**

Philistines—the neighbours next door—came from the west and were the coastal people on the eastern seaboard of the Mediterranean; the modern name 'Palestine' derives from them. The biblical record identifies the Philistines as the descendants of Casluhim from the line of Ham (Genesis 10:14).

57
Ancient
Near East

Abraham and Isaac both confronted Abimelech of Philistia (Genesis 20 and 26) and throughout the history of Israel the Philistines were the aggressive next door neighbours, though they never managed to build an empire. Significantly Israel avoided the land of the Philistines when they journeyed out from Egypt (Exodus 13:17). It was in one of the many local conflicts with their neighbour that young David slew Goliath, a Philistine from Gath (1 Samuel 17: 48–51).

Syrians—the neighbours up north—were Israel's immediate northern neighbours whose

Above: Phoenician ivory (WA127412). A lioness killing a Nubian (Nubia is now Sudan) against a backing of lillies and papyrus flowers originally inlaid with lapislazuli (blue) and carnelian (red), with gold foil

Facing page : A Phoenician ivoy panel (ANE 118418) showing a figure wearing royal Egyptian-style garments. From the palace of Ashurnasirpal II

(Height of both: 8cm)

Hebrew kings: The kingdom divided—Israel and Judah

Only those kings mentioned in this guide are listed here. Co-regencies are not shown. Those marked with an asterisk are also referred to in contemporary documents outside the Bible.

Judah (20 kings reigning in Jerusalem)   **Israel** (20 kings reigning in Samaria)

	BC		BC
Rehoboam	930–913	Jeroboam I	930–909
Asa	910–870	Baasha	908–886
		Omri*	885–874
Jehoshaphat	870–848	Ahab*	874–853
Joash*	835–796	Jehu*	841–814
		sent tribute to Assyria in 841.	
		Jehoahaz	814–798
Amaziah	796–767	Jeroboam II	782–753
		Menahem*	752–742
Ahaz	732–716	Hoshea*	732–723
		Fall of Samaria to Assyria (722).	
Hezekiah*	716–687	Sennacherib attacked Jerusalem in 701.	
Manasseh*	687–642		
Josiah	640–609		
Jehoahaz*	609		
Jehoiakim*	609–597	Many Jews exiled to Babylon including Daniel and Ezekiel.	
Zedekiah	597–587	Fall of Jerusalem to Babylon (16 March 597). More Jews into exile. Final destruction in 587.	
	539	The fall of Babylon to Persia, and Cyrus of Persia allows Jews to return and rebuild Jerusalem.	
	516	The Temple completed. Prophets Haggai and Zechariah.	
	458	Ezra in Jerusalem.	
	445	Nehemiah in Jerusalem. Malachi and close of OT.	

For list of Babylonian kings see page 50. Persian kings page 60. Egyptian kings page 69. Assyrian kings page 84. Roman Emperors page 102.

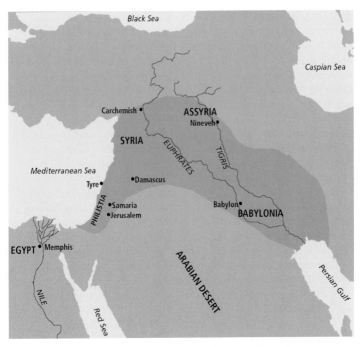

Israel's neighbours in the time of the kings of Israel and Judah

territory ran from the Euphrates down to the Sea of Galilee. The word 'Syrian' cannot be used of a political unit before the Seleucid kings of the 4th century BC; prior to that they were properly known as Aramaeans whose ancestry is traced back in Genesis 10:22 to Shem. It was from this line that Abraham was descended, giving rise to the reference in Deuteronomy 26:5 that when the Israelites entered Canaan they were to declare, 'A wandering Aramaean was my father.' King David married an Aramaean princess who gave birth to Absalom (2 Samuel 3:3). In the latter years of Solomon a renegade, Rezon, established himself at Damascus and this

became the capital of southern Syria. From here on Syria was a troublesome northern neighbour who, after the division of the monarchy between Israel in the north and Judah in the south (in 931 BC), often either attacked or sided with Israel against Judah.

Babylonians—distant neighbours. They lived to the east of the Aramaeans in modern day Iraq. They are referred to in Genesis 10:10 under the title 'the land of Shinar', whilst in Jeremiah 24:5 we find another common description: 'the land of the Chaldeans'. From a biblical viewpoint the most well-known of all Babylonian kings was the mighty Nebuchanezzar (also Nebuchadrezzar) who, at the

Battle of Carchemish in 605 BC destroyed the Egyptian army and made himself master of an empire reaching from the border of modern day Iran right down to Egypt. In the middle of this mayhem, Ezekiel, Daniel and his young friends were taken into exile to Babylon.

The Assyrians to the north were also threatening neighbours and we will meet them in chapter 6 on page 81.

When we move from Room 56 to **Room 57 Ancient Near East** we are making a significant jump forward in time. This area is sometimes referred to as 'the Levant'. Immediately on your right are some particularly interesting exhibits.

Post-it notes

The *Lachish Letters* in *case 10* on your right as you enter the room.

These messages, scrawled on scraps of broken pottery, were written when Babylon was invading Judah in 587 BC. Such texts are known as 'ostraca'—the equivalent of today's scrap paper. The prophet Jeremiah refers to the devastation caused by Nebuchadnezzar as his terrifying Babylonian army swept across Palestine in the time of King Zedekiah of Judah (587 BC— 2 Kings 25). Jeremiah refers to Lachish and Azekah as the only remaining fortified cities before Jerusalem itself is attacked (Jeremiah 34:7). Don't confuse this with the defeat of Lachish by Sennacherib in 701 BC that we will meet later in our tour (see pages 88–90).

One of these messages is particularly interesting. It is the top right ostracon on the panel *(WA125702)*. This was found with

Above: Lachish ostracon (WA125702). A hastily scribbled message as the Babylonian army advances on Jerusalem in the time of Zedekiah. Height: 9cm

Above: Inscription of a royal steward to Hezekiah?(WA125205). This is possibly the Shebna of Isaiah 22

the others in the shattered gatehouse of Lachish and is a note from an officer of an outpost to his commanding officer in Lachish (see Jeremiah 34:7). It contains the divine name Yahweh (LORD) when he writes in haste: 'May Yahweh cause my lord to hear news of peace, even now, even now'. Yahweh is the first word at the right hand end of the second line down. (Hebrew reads from right to left.)

The message includes the words: 'Who is your servant but a dog that my lord should remember his servant?'—this is an interesting echo of 2 Samuel 9:8; 16:9 and 2 Kings 8:13.

Another message closes with the ominous words: 'We are watching for the beacon from Lachish, following the signals you, sir, gave, but we do not see Azekah.' Azekah was 15 kilometres (9 miles) north of Lachish. It is a frantic and futile hope; the cities are falling and only these two are left before Jerusalem itself falls to the devastating armies of Nebuchadnezzar.

You will find it helpful to read the board entitled *Israel and Judah*.

Do not disturb

Above the board *Chronology*—to the left of the doorway you have just entered—is an ***inscribed lintel of a rock-cut tomb*** in Jerusalem *(WA125205)*; this is very likely the steward referred to in Isaiah 22:15–19.

Shebna is in trouble because as a steward in the household of King Hezekiah of Judah, he is living above his station; apparently he has carved out a tomb for himself in a very conspicuous place and inscribed it with his own name. Though the first part of the name is missing it is most likely the Shebna whom Isaiah denounced for his arrogance. The inscription tells us that there is nothing of value in his tomb except his bones and those of his maidservant.

On the extreme right hand end of *case 10* is a pink ***limestone seal from Lachish*** *(WA 12011)* 'belonging to Shebna, son of Ahab'. This may well be the Shebna of Isaiah's prophecy; in which case his father Ahab is not Ahab the King of Israel because Shebna is steward to the King of Judah! However, both names are fairly common.

Above: Three of the Amarna letters. EA29832 is on the right (no. 3)

Who are these Hapiru?

The Amarna letters are part of a collection of 380 tablets that were discovered from 1887 at El-Amarna in Egypt. They are letters from various subject rulers to the Pharaohs of Egypt Amenhotep III and Amenhotep IV (later Akhenaten see List of Egyptian kings on page 69 and Egyptian king list page 79) in the 14th century BC when Egyptian power was beginning to decline. The letters contain increasingly desperate pleas for assistance against the growing strength of homeless groups. Especially they refer to the *Hapiru*. The clay tablet *EA 29832* is from the ruler at Gezer and includes the plea: 'May the king, my lord, the sun in the sky, care for his land. Since the *Hapiru* are stronger than us, may the king, my lord, help me escape from the *Hapiru*, so that the *Hapiru* do not destroy us.' Just who these *Hapiru* were has been much debated. Some think that *Hapiru* was the name given to marauding bands generally, of which the Hebrews were part. However, if we accept an early date for the Exodus (see page 70), the appeal in the Amarna letters for help against these people would fit well the period of conquest under Joshua and the Judges.

Notice the weights in *case 10* (beside the Shebna seal) **Weights from Lachish**.

These weights from the time of Isaiah and Hezekiah are in shekels; before coins were minted, payments were made by weighing silver bullion (see page 104). It is now known that the Hebrew word *payim* (1 Samuel 13:21) is one third of a shekel, because the word *payim* is engraved on one of the weights here.

Taxes and more taxes. Also in *case 10* (below) notice the handles broken from storage jars *(WA132061 on)*. These come from Lachish possibly in the time of King Hezekiah (716–687 BC) and they are stamped 'Belonging to the King'. The cities of Hebron, Ziph, Socoh and Mamshit are each mentioned and these may have been administrative centres where taxes to the king were brought.

Case 9 is an introduction to the *Philistines* (see above page 39).

The *Amarna letters* in *case 8* were written from Canaan to the Pharaoh of Egypt possibly at a time when the Hebrews were entering the land. Some refer to *Hapiru,* and this may be an early reference to the Hebrew invaders. See Box: Who are these Hapiru? (facing page).

The dung beetle!

Continuing to your left, in *case 7* you will find *scarabs (WA 1980-12-14 on)*. These are replicas of the dung beetle and you will notice them often throughout our tour. They are found first in Egypt 2300 years BC and became popular as amulets and a mark of ownership.

Above: A scarab (dung beetle) representing resurrection and life—similar to the one on display

Although they are not mentioned in the Bible, they were commonly used as good luck charms. It was generally thought that the dung beetle (rolling a ball of dung in front of it) represented the sun god pushing the sun across the sky. As the dung contains the beetle's larvae and various seeds, it became an emblem of resurrection and new life.

Ivory houses and a crime writer

Move across to the opposite wall *case 12* Nimrud for the *Phoenician Ivory*. See pictures on pages 38–39.

This is a sample of the way luxurious furniture was decorated by kings across the ancient Near East. From the time of King Solomon ivory was a symbol of wealth in Israel (1 Kings 10:18 refers to an ivory throne overlaid with gold), and when the monarchy divided, both Israel and Judah squandered their riches in this way. See the reference to Ahab's ivory palace (1 Kings 22:39). His wife, Jezebel, was a Phoenician princess and much of the ivory carving was done by Phoenician craftsmen copying Egyptian designs. The white of the ivory was enhanced by coloured gemstone inlays and gold foil plating. Excavations in the ruins of Israelite palaces at Samaria revealed hundreds of pieces of intricately carved ivory. It is possible that many of these date from the time of Ahab about 860 BC. However, a more likely dating would locate them in the mid 8th century in the time of Azariah (Uzziah) of Judah and Jeroboam II of Israel. It was this wasteful luxury that the prophet Amos vigorously condemned in his preaching at this time. Amos 3:15 records, 'The houses adorned with

Above: Agatha Christie at an archaeological dig in north-east Syria in the 1930s

Agatha Christie and the ivories

Agatha Christie's second husband, Max Mallowan, was a noted archaeologist and the renowned crime writer travelled extensively with him. On some of the digs she helped clean a number of the ivories now on display, including the ivory of a lioness killing a Nubian (No.7 WA127412 see page 39). The theme is Egyptian in origin and symbolises the king triumphing over his enemies. Max wrote about her work at Nimrud: 'Agatha's controlled imagination came to our aid. She instantly realized that objects which had lived under water for 2000 years had to be nursed back into a new and relatively arid climate.' Describing the cleaning process Agatha wrote: 'I had my own favourite tools, just as any professional would: an orange stick, possibly a very fine knitting needle—one season a dentist's tool which he lent, or rather gave me—and a jar of cosmetic face-cream, which I found more useful than anything else for gently coaxing the dirt out of crevices without harming the friable ivory. In fact there was such a run on my face cream that there was nothing left for my poor old face after a couple of weeks.'

Some of her books inspired by archaeology include: *A Murder in Mesopotamia* and *Death on the Nile.*

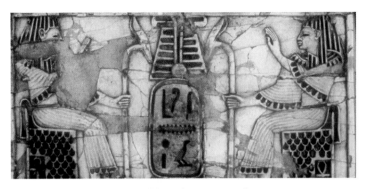

Above: An ivory plaque carved by a Phoenician craftsman imitating Egyptian style. 8th century BC (WA 118 120)
Below: An example of intricate Phoenician ivory from the time of Ahab and Jezebel or a century later in the time of Amos: 'Woman at the window'— reminiscent of Jezebel's death (WA118156)

ivory will be destroyed', and 6:4 pronounces a woe on those who 'lie on beds inlaid with ivory'. Even later than this, among the items of tribute that the Assyrian king Sennacherib claims Hezekiah sent to him at Nineveh are 'ivory-decorated beds and ivory-decorated armchairs, elephant hide and tusks…'

Note the **woman at the window** *(no.9 WA118156)*; Jezebel met her death in a scene reminiscent of this (2 Kings 9:30).

In the left corner just before you enter Room 58 there is a large storage pot from Hazor *(WA132309)*, dated around 1400 BC which could be in the time of Joshua (Joshua 11:10).

Bones and boundary stones
Enter **Room 58** and on your left is a *burial chamber from Jericho* dated somewhere in the Middle Bronze Age (between 2000 and 1550 BC). This is laid out as it was found, and from the artefacts buried with the dead it was clearly owned by a wealthy family. The custom of burying members of a family together is reflected in the tomb of Abraham, Sarah and their descendants at Hebron (Genesis.23:17–20; 49:29–32; 50:13).

Return back through **Rooms 57** and **56** and enter **Room 55**—Ancient Near East
Cases 1 (immediately in front of you) and 2 (to your left) provide an interesting display of *Stone Kudurru*. These were of great importance in the ancient world—see Proverbs 22:28, 'Do not remove an ancient boundary stone set up by your forefathers' and Hosea 5:10. To move a boundary stone ('landmark') was

The Taylor Prism

The king begins by introducing himself: 'Sennacherib, the great King, the powerful King, the King of Assyria, the unrivalled, the pious monarch, the worshipper of the great gods. The protector of the just; the lover of the righteous, the noble warrior, the valiant hero, the first of all the Kings, the great punisher of unbelievers who are breakers of the holy festivals. Ashur, the great lord, had given me an unrivalled monarchy. Over all princes he has raised triumphantly my arms.' He then describes his defeat of the king of Babylon (Merodach-Baladan referred to in 2 Kings 20 and Isaiah 39) and the wholesale slaughter and pillaging that followed. Little wonder that 2 Kings 18:13–16 records Hezekiah's vain attempt to pay off Sennacherib by stripping the Temple of its gold. When Sennacherib finally arrived at the walls of Jerusalem he had already laid waste across Judah forty-six 'strong cities, fortresses, and small cities which were round them' and had 'captured 200,150 people, small and great, male and female'. His were no idle threats (vs 28–35). However, Isaiah stiffened the defenders' resistance (19:20–34), assuring them of victory and even warning the king of Assyria that God would treat him as cruelly as he treated his captives (v 28). In his own record Sennacherib adds that, 'The terrifying splendour of my majesty overcame Hezekiah. The elite forces and his good soldiers he had brought in to strengthen his royal city Jerusalem, did not fight.' According to verses 35–37 they did not need to! The king then lists the tribute that Hezekiah had sent to him. Sennacherib withdrew and returned home where history records that he was assassinated some years later.

Above: *The Taylor Prism (WA 91032). The detail outlined in white describes how Sennacherib shut up Hezekiah in Jerusalem, 'like a caged bird'. Later the text describes the tribute Hezekiah sent Sennacherib. (Height: 38.5cm)*

Above: This boundary stone (WA 102485) records a gift of land, which is carefully defined; the carvings are emblems of the gods called upon to curse anyone who challenges the ownership of the property or defaces the stone (c.1125–1100 BC) (Height 37cm)

nothing short of stealing a man's land and this deserved the judgement of God.

In Babylonia, boundary stones were known as *kudurru* and they acted as legal documents; it is possible that clay copies were kept on the property because these more durable carvings on stone were all discovered in temples—the bank vaults of the day.

A bird in a cage—an interlude in Assyria

Continue to *case 11* on the left of the room. Here is *The Taylor Prism (WA91032)* which is Sennacherib's own description of his siege of Jerusalem in the time of Hezekiah. See Box on List of Assyrian kings page 84 and the Box: The Taylor Prism on the facing page.

This exhibit is out of historical sequence at this point, but to examine it now will save returning later. By the time Hezekiah came to the throne of Judah in 716, Samaria in the north was already under the control of Assyria. Hezekiah's father, Ahaz, had made Judah a vassal state of Assyria, but Hezekiah decided to assert his independence and seek support from Egypt. When Sennacherib succeeded his father, Sargon, he turned his attention to Jerusalem. The details of what followed are recorded in 2 Kings 18–19, 2 Chronicles 32, and Isaiah 36–37.

Sennacherib left his own account on this six-sided clay prism. It was discovered in 1830 at Nineveh by Colonel Geoffrey Taylor, the British Resident in Baghdad, and is therefore known as The Taylor Prism. It records the first eight military campaigns of Sennacherib, but it is the account of his third campaign, in the year 701 BC, that is of interest to us. Having defeated the Phoenicians and received tribute from Moab and Edom, he intercepted an Egyptian force on its way to the relief of Jerusalem. Hezekiah had

Babylonian kings

	BC	
Nabopolassar	626–605	Babylon competing for domination.
Nebuchadrezzar II*	605–562	605 defeat of Egypt at Carchemish. Babylonian supremacy. See Jeremiah 46:2
	606	Jehoiakim of Judah became a vassal of Nebuchadnezzar (2 Kings 24:1) and Daniel taken into exile. 587 Jerusalem captured, Temple destroyed and its treasures taken to Babylon (Daniel 1:1–2).
	597	Jehoiachin and Ezekiel taken to Babylon.
Amel-Marduk*	562–560	Evil-Merodach of 2 Kings 25:27, Jews still in exile.
Nergal-Shar-usur*	560–556	Nergal-Sharezar of Jeremiah 39:3, Jews still in exile.
Labashi-Marduk	556	Jews still in exile.
Nabonidus	556–539	Belshazzar* son of Nabonidus, as co-regent. (Daniel 5:22).

Babylon captured by Persia in 539 and the end of an empire.

Note: Daniel served in the royal courts of the last five kings of Babylon and Cyrus of Persia.

* These kings are mentioned by name in the Bible

For list of Hebrew kings page 40. Persian kings page 60. Egyptian kings page 69. Assyrian kings page 84. Roman Emperors page 102.

made a treaty with Egypt which proved to be a 'broken reed' (2 Kings 18:19–21). Sennacherib records that he shut up Hezekiah in his royal city 'like a caged bird'. In the event, it was Lachish and not Jerusalem that adorned the walls of his victory room in Nineveh, as we shall see. See pages 88–90.

Also in *case 11* is a **Stela of Ashurbanipal** (WA90865, WA90864) the grandson of Sennacherib. He is the king referred to under the Aramaic 'Osnapper' in Ezra 4:10, (NIV translates 'Ashurbanipal') and who released Manasseh from his prison exile in Babylon referred to in 2 Chronicles 33:10–13. See also page 93.

In the panel to the left are two letters to Esarhaddon (WAK8681, WAK135586) king of Assyria and son of Sennacherib (see 2 Kings 19:37 and Isaiah 37:38). Below are clay and stone records (WA78223, WA91027) on which Esarhaddon, a great builder, records how he restored the city of Babylon that his father had destroyed.

Back to Babylon

Continue to *case 12* where you will find a display of **The world of Nebuchadnezzar**.

Nebuchadnezzar (sometimes spelt Nebuchadrezzar) was the major player on the world stage during the final years of Judah, and he was the ruler who destroyed the city of Jerusalem and brought the line of the Judean kings to an end with the capture of Zedekiah in 587 BC. The first mention of him in the Bible is in 2 Kings 24:1, but he is mentioned frequently by Jeremiah (e.g. 25:1) and Ezekiel

Above: A brick c. 605BC with the following cuneiform inscription: 'Nebuchadrezzar, King of Babylon ... the eldest son of Nabolpolassar King of Babylon, am I.' From a private collection. Length 33cm

You can find more bricks from the time of Nebuchadrezzar, and earlier from ancient Ur, in Room 1 (The King's Library— The Enlightenment). Enter from the Great Court and turn left past the facsimile of the Rosetta Stone

Above: *The Cylinder of Nabonidus which refers to King Belshazzar (WA91128) (Length: 10.4cm)*

The Nabonidus Cylinder

Nabonidus was the last king of Babylon, and Daniel lived through his reign. Nabonidus, who is not referred to by name in the Bible, restored two temples of the moon god Sin. In 1854 J E Taylor, the British Consul in Basra, was exploring the ruins of the ancient ziggurat at Tell el Muqayyar (ancient Ur of the Chaldees) in southern Iraq when he discovered at the corners four identical clay 'time capsules'. They had been placed there by Nabonidus and on each he recounts the history of the ziggurat and adds a prayer for the long life and good health of himself and 'Belshazzar, my firstborn son, the offspring of my heart.' In response to an omen, Nabonidus spent many years at the oasis of Teima in north-west Arabia, and Belshazzar remained at Babylon as co-regent and thus as de facto king. This is why Daniel 5:1 refers to him as the King, and v 29 states that Daniel was proclaimed 'third highest ruler in the kingdom'. This dual reign also explains why v 30 says that the night on which the Persians broke into the city of Babylon: 'Belshazzar, king of the Babylonians, was slain', whereas the records of the Persian king Cyrus claims that he took the King of Babylon (Nabonidus) prisoner (see the *Cyrus Cylinder* later in Room 52 page 64).

(e.g. 26:7), and was responsible for the exile of Daniel who has much to say about him in Daniel 1–4. Ezra and Nehemiah also refer to him.

Central to this case is a reconstructed wall of the glazed bricks that once adorned the ziggurat at Ur (see page 26), and other glazed bricks of the period.

It is this glazing that necessitated the very hot furnaces recorded in Daniel 3:6.

Notice here also the *Temple of the Sun*, this is the ziggurat of the sun god Shamash. Many of the items here are from the ruins of this temple.

The information board is well worth reading. The exhibits here

Above: Rembrandt's Belshazzar's Feast

Below: A fragment of coloured glazed brick from the throne room in Babylon where Belshazzar held his feast (from a private collection)

all refer to the period when Babylon and Assyria were jockeying for power. They were major powers in the history of Israel. God's warning to Israel that he would bring judgement from the north (e.g. Jeremiah 1:14–15; 4:6; 10:22) generally refers to Babylon. You gain here some idea of the magnificent city of Babylon in the time of Jeremiah, Ezekiel and Daniel. The reference on this board to 'ancient stories suggesting that Nebuchadnezzar became mad' reflects the biblical account in Daniel 4.

In *case 14* (to your right at the back of *case 13*) there are many examples of clay cylinders commemorating the reconstruction and repairs to temples by Nebuchadnezzar— see WA91142, WA91137. Also here is a brick of Nebuchadnezzar (WA90081) which is part of one of his many building works intended to proclaim his name to posterity; it reminds us of his boast: 'Is not this the great Babylon I have built as the royal residence, by my mighty power and for the glory of my majesty?' (Daniel 4:30).

The king who never lived?

The *Cylinder of Nabonidus in case 14 (WA91128)* gives substance to the words 'King Belshazzar' in Daniel 5:1 which, until 1854, was the only known reference to this king and was thought by one scholar to be 'a figment of the writer's imagination'. It is now known that he was the son of Nabonidus, and co-regent in Babylon. See Box: The Nabonidus Cylinder on page 52.

In *case 16* in the centre at the far end of the room notice *The East India House Inscription (WA129397)* which records the devotion and achievements of Nebuchadnezzar. The reference to the god Marduk in part reads: 'Create in my heart the worship of your divinity and grant whatever is pleasing to you because you have fashioned my life.' It is a good example of cuneiform writing.

Especially read the information board *The Stela of Nabonidus* on the end wall. The details here fit precisely the evidence from the book of Daniel.

Chronicle including the first Babylonian capture of Jerusalem in *case 15 (no. 24 WA21946)* is one of a series of clay tablets that list the main events of the Babylonian kings. This tablet (often referred to as a 'Babylonian Chronicle') covers

Above: Part of the East India House Inscription which expresses the devotion and achievements of Nebuchadnezzar in clear cuneiform script. (WA129397)

Right: The Babylonian Chronicle (WA21946) which may be displayed showing the obverse, and will therefore appeear upside down. The text (highlighted here) reads that the King:

'encamped against the city of Judah and on the second day of the month Adar, he seized the city and captured the king (this was Jehoiachin). He appointed there a king of his own choice (Zedekiah), received its heavy tribute and sent (them) to Babylon'.

(Height: 6cm)

the years 605–595 from the decisive battle of Carchemish (Jeremiah 46:2). It records that in the seventh year of Nebuchadnezzar he marched into 'Hatti-land' (Syria-Palestine) and camped against 'the city of Judah' (Jerusalem). Tells how he captured the city and its king, received tribute and appointed his own king. See 2 Kings 24:8–17. The Chronicle's careful dating fixes the date for the fall of Jerusalem under Jehoiachin as 16 March 597 BC. The Chronicle does not mention by name either Jehoiachin or his puppet successor Zedekiah.

Notice also the **plaque of the dragon** (WA103381) which represents the god Marduk and *no.25* the **Prayer to Marduk** of the man in prison (WA40474).

A Scrabble cheat in the King's court

On the opposite wall in *case 10* there are clay documents from the Assyrian library in Nineveh relating to the time of Sargon, Sennacherib and Ashurbanipal kings of Assyria—we will meet these kings again later. In *column 1* a document recounts the legend of how an earlier Sargon (2340–2284 BC) was discovered as a baby in a basket floating on the river *(WAK3401)*. Also included here is **The Flood Tablet** *(WAK3375)*. See Box: The Gilgamesh Epic on page 56. Also here notice: **The Epic of Creation** *(WAK3473)*.

If you have time you will enjoy looking in this case for many other fascinating documents of the time from the royal libraries at

Nineveh, including: the scrabble cheat from the library of Ashurbanipal *column 2 (WAK4375)*; *column 4* the ominous end of a substitute king: if the omens told of imminent danger to the king, a substitute would be put on the throne and executed when the danger had passed—unless the danger killed him first! *(WAK2600)*; and on the bottom row, a plea from a failed scholar *(WAK4267)* and a hymn to the goddess Ishtar *(WAASm954)*.

Walk into **Room 54** and notice in passing (*case 5* in centre of the room) information about the Hittites who we will meet in the next room. Enter **Room 53 Ancient Near east**

Hittites and run!

Here in **Room 53** we have a glimpse of the *Hittites*. Before the late 19th century the only known reference to the Hittites was in the Bible. Abraham purchased a burial site for Sarah from Hittite merchants (Genesis 23), and Joshua 1:4 describes their land in what we know as Syria. Their ancient capital of Hattusha was discovered in 1906. The Hittite empire was founded c1700 BC but by 1200 BC their power was broken. However, the descendants of the Hittites still ruled some places in the time of David: Hamath (2 Samuel 8:9) was a Hittite city, David's kingdom bordered Hittite territory (Tahtim Hodshi of 2 Samuel 24:6?), and Bathsheba's Hittite husband was one of David's military officers (2 Samuel 11:3). Solomon married a Hittite (1 Kings 11:1) and sold on horses to them (1 Kings 10:29). In the time of Ahab (874–853 BC) a possible coalition between Hittites and Egypt could terrify the armies of Ben Hadad, King of Aram:

The Gilgamesh Epic—a story of a flood

Discovered by George Smith in 1872, this is the story of Gilgamesh who seeks immortality. He meets Utnapishtim who tells how he gained immortality by surviving the flood. There are interesting similarities, though wide divergences also, with the biblical record. Utnapishtim is instructed by the god Ea to build a great boat and bring his family and representatives of all living creatures into it. They ride out a terrible flood that destroys the rest of mankind. Utnapishtim finally sends out a dove, a swallow and a raven—the raven does not return. Together with his family and menagerie, Utnapishtim leaves the boat on Mount Nisir in what is now Kurdistan, and offers sacrifices to the gods. He and his wife are given immortality. These accounts, and there are other flood stories from the ancient world, at least point to the fact that stories of creation and a great flood were common in the world of Abraham. This tablet is dated around 650 BC but is clearly a copy of a much older original. Compare Box: The Babylonian story of the Flood—the Atrahasis Epic on page 32.

*Above: The storm god, Baal, worshipped by the Hittites and other nations. Israel often mixed her worship of the L*ORD *with that of Baal—see for example 1 Kings 18:18 (WA 117909)*

'Look, the King of Israel has hired the Hittite and Egyptian kings to attack us!" So they got up and fled … and ran for their lives' (2 Kings 7:6–7).

As you enter **Room 53**, immediately on your right is a relief of the storm god *(WA 117909)* who was worshipped as Teshub by the Hittites; in Canaan this was the god Baal who is frequently mentioned in the Old Testament. Because he was the god of the storm it was all the more significant that Baal was defeated by fire from heaven on a clear day, in the contest on Carmel (1 Kings 18:20–40).

As the Hittite power declined, they contracted to the area of Carchemish (see board *The Neo-Hittite States*). Carchemish was taken first by the Assyrians in 717 BC, then by Egypt in 609 BC, and finally by Nebuchadnezzar of Babylon in 605 BC when he defeated the forces of Pharaoh Neco. Jeremiah 46:2 refers to this battle, as does the Babylonian Chronicle that we saw earlier in *Room 55 case 15* (page 54 and 55).

The case on the left contains arrowheads from Carchemish (*WA116191*) where fierce battles were fought. Above are small Egyptian gods (*WA116184*) reflecting the struggle for influence as the Hittite power collapsed. The copy of a relief at the top of the wall shows the royal Hittite children with their games.

Turn right into **Room 52 Ancient Near East.**

❹ Persia—land of the Great Kings

A new and more powerful empire arose. Bandits provide us with an insight into the fabulous wealth of this mighty empire in the time of Esther—an empire that eclipsed those of Assyria and Babylon. A great road from Sardis in Turkey to Susa in Iran enabled the first Royal Mail route to keep the empire informed of the King's edicts. This was truly the first world Empire

Room 52 Ancient Near East

A Persian Queen

The Persians probably originated from southern Russia and their main cities were Ecbatana, Susa, Pasargadae and Persepolis, all in modern day Iran. They came late in the history of the Old Testament, and we meet them first in 2 Chronicles 36:20, 'the kingdom of Persia came to power.' In October 539 BC the armies of Cyrus II entered and destroyed Babylon and heralded the great Medio-Persian Empire.

In Daniel 5:31 we read, 'Darius the Mede took over the kingdom'; this is either an alternative royal title for Cyrus, or a reference to a subordinate—possibly Gubaru who was known to have governed Babylon for Cyrus. Cyrus ruled his vast empire—from India to North Afica—from his capital at Susa. Here, sixty years later, Esther was queen to Xerxes. See Esther 1:12; 2:16–17.

Persia remained the new world power until Alexander the Great of Macedonia defeated the Great King Darius III in 331 BC.

Cyrus, Darius, Xerxes (Ahaseurus), and Artaxerxes were the Persian kings of the latter part of the life of Daniel, the history of Esther and the return to Jerusalem as recorded in Ezra, Nehemiah and the prophets Haggai, Zechariah and Malachi.

The Greek historian, Herodotus, wrote his *Histories* in the same century when Esther was Queen in Susa; to possess a work of history from the same time, although from a Greek perspective, is valuable. Translations of Herodotus' book can be purchased from the Museum bookshop.

Facing page: The beautiful panel of glazed brick from Susa in the time of Esther (WA132525)

Persian kings

	BC	
Achaemenes	c.700–675	Founded Persian kingdom and the Achaemenid dynasty.
Cyrus I	c.640–600	Persia not yet a world power.
Cyrus II*	559–530	Established Persian dominance and captured Babylon. Jews return to Jerusalem and rebuild Temple. Ezra 1:1–4.
Cambyses II	530–522	Jews becoming re-established in their homeland.
Darius I*	522–486	Extended the empire into northern India and ranged into Europe. Temple completed. Persian Wars failed to subdue the Greeks. Haggai and Zechariah prophesying.
Xerxes I*	486–465	Ahaserus* in the Bible. Lost Persian Wars and the decline of Empire began. Esther was one of his queens.
Artaxerxes I*	465–424	Ezra sent to Jerusalem by the King (Ezra 7:1). Nehemiah his cupbearer (Nehemiah 1:11).
Darius II	424–404	Post-biblical
Darius III	336–330	Defeated by Alexander the Great and end of Persian Empire.

* These kings are mentioned by name in the Bible
For list of Hebrew kings page 40. Babylonian kings page 50. Egyptian kings page 69. Assyrian kings page 84. Roman Emperors page 102.

Left: Herodotus (c. 484–425 BC) Greek historian, known as 'the Father of History'

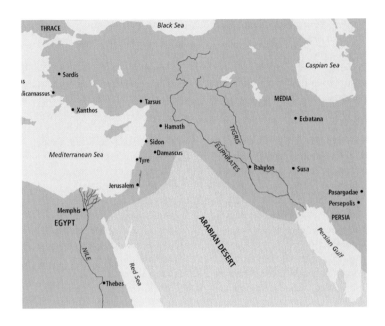

The extent of the Persian Empire

Bricks and bandits

Facing you as you enter **Room 52** is a colourful *panel of glazed brick* showing a guard on duty *(WA132525)* see picture on page 58. This once adorned the palace at Susa of Darius I, the Great King of Persia (522–486 BC). He is referred to in Ezra 4:5; 5:6–7; 6:1; Haggai 1:1 and Zechariah 1:1. Perhaps the royal guards, Bigthan and Teresh in Esther 2:21, were dressed like this.

Darius built a magnificent palace at Susa and you can imagine the splendour of a building decorated with wall panels like these. His son was Xerxes (486–465 BC), the king referred to in the Bible as Ahaseurus (Esther 1:1 Xerxes). This would have been the palace that Esther was familiar with when she became queen. Nehemiah was cupbearer to the king in this great city just two or three decades after Esther was queen (Nehemiah 1:1,11).

In *cases 27–29* in the centre of the room you will find the **Oxus Treasure** see Box: Burton and the bandits on page 62. This comes from the same period and illustrates the exquisite jewellery and other items of Esther's time. Persia was fabulously wealthy and when Alexander destroyed Susa in December 331 BC it is claimed that he found 1,180 tons of gold, and a further 300 tons at Persepolis in January 330 BC. Follow round these central cases to gain an idea of the wealth of

Esther's court. Notice especially the *gold drinking cup* (*WA123921*), a reminder of the banquet in the royal court recorded in Esther 1:7 'Wine was served in goblets of gold'. In *case 29* below the map there is beautiful gold jewellery.

At the far end of this room you will see stone carvings from the Palace at Persepolis that Darius began and Xerxes completed. Here there are guards, officials and chariots. Though Persepolis was geographically at some distance from Susa, it is a good example of the architecture, costumes etc that would have been familiar to Esther. Read Esther 1:3–7 to gain an impression of the lavish splendour of the Persian court.

In *case 20 to your right* you will find impressive swords of the time. Note that the helmets here are Assyrian and not Persian; they are depicted in the Lachish Relief that we will see later in Room 10 (pages 88–91).

Return across the room to *case 25* and notice the Babylonian observation of Halley's Comet (*WA41462*) which can be dated to about 22–28 September 164 BC. This is included here as an illustration of one way to fix early dating very accurately.

In *case 8 (top left)* notice the

Burton and the bandits—The story of the Oxus Treasure

Three merchants travelling to India were passing through Afghanistan in May 1880 with a large hoard of gold and silver that had been found on the north bank of the Oxus river. They were attacked and robbed by bandits, but their servant managed to escape and alerted the local British political officer, Cap. F.C.Burton. Burton went in pursuit, caught up with the robbers and persuaded them to return a significant portion of the merchants' belongings. In a bag that had been cut open, a magnificent gold bracelet was discovered, which Burton later

bought. The merchants had been carrying over 170 objects from the Achaemenid period and 1,500 coins from the early fifth to the third centuries BC. This made up what you see here as the Oxus treasure. The merchants sold much of the treasure in Rawalpindi (Northeast Pakistan) to Major General Sir Alexander Cunningham who was Director General of the Archaeological Survey of India. Eventually this valuable collection was passed to the British Museum.

Pictured: *A gold armband from Persia in the time of Esther (WA 124017) (Width: 10cm)*

Above: An intricate gold chariot from Persia in the time of Esther (WA123908) (Length: 9cm)

calcite vase (WA1857–12–20) from the time of Darius I. It is inscribed in four languages.

Returning home

As you return back down the hall look at *case 6* on your right. It contains *The Cyrus Cylinder* (WA90920)—see picture on page 64—an interesting document proclaiming that King Cyrus of Persia (559–529 BC) allowed exiles taken captive during the time of the Babylonian empire to return to their own country and rebuild their temples—often with help from the Persian exchequer!

According to 2 Chronicles 36:23 and Ezra 1:2–4 Cyrus king of Persia claimed that he had been

Above: A gold jug from Susa in the time of Esther (WA 123918/OT17) Height: 14cm

Above: The Cyrus Cylinder (WA90920) which records the policy of Cyrus, King of Persia, allowing exiles to return to their homes and rebuild their cities and temples. Length: 16cm

Above: A seal of Darius I, during whose reign Haggai and Zechariah were prophecying. The title of Darius in the text to the left is written in three languages. Above the King is the winged-disk emblem of Ahuramazda, the national god of ancient Persia. Length: 5.5cm

Above: The magnificent walls at Persepolis

charged by: 'The LORD, the God of heaven' to build a house for him at Jerusalem. Cyrus gave permission for the Jews in exile to return to their city and rebuild both the city and 'the temple of the LORD, the God of Israel, the God who is in Jerusalem'. This cylinder describes his victory over Babylon in 539 BC and how he returned a number of the national gods to their temples and arranged for people who had been taken into exile to return home. The cylinder does not refer to the Jews by name, but it confirms the policy described in Ezra 6:3–5. In part it reads: 'I am Cyrus, king of all, the great king, the mighty king, king of Babylon, king of Sumer and Akkad, king of the four corners of the earth…'

Also here in *case 6* is the ***King in his chariot shoots at a lion***; this is a seal of the Great King Darius I (*WA 89132*) referred to above. It is inscribed in three languages.

Look below for ***Hero fights human headed bull***; this is a seal of Parshandata (WA89152), and although there is no reason to assume it is the same person, the name is found in Esther 9:7, showing that it was a familiar name of the time.

No. 4 **A table of eclipses** (*WA32234*) is of interest because it refers to the murder of Xerxes by his son on 14 August 465 BC. There is no record of the fate of Esther.

Nos 6,7 and *8* illustrate the extent of the Persian Empire in the time of Cyrus from Egypt to Ur in Mesopotamia.

No.9 is a fine example of ***glazed bricks*** from the palace at Susa.

Return to **Room 53** and continue straight ahead into **Room 65—Early Egypt.**

⑤ Return to Egypt

An exotic land full of mummies, myths and monuments, beloved by authors and film makers because of Pyramids, romance, adventure and fabulous discoveries. Marvel at the skill of the craftsman and learn something of this ancient culture

Room 65—Egypt

Black land—Red land

'Egypt is the gift of the Nile' according to the ancient Greek historian Herodotus. Egypt owed to the Nile its security, prosperity, religion and even its calendar—the three seasons of the Egyptian year were governed by the flow of the river. One of the earliest civilizations known to man, the ancient Egyptians called their land by two names: *kemet* (black land), referring to the black mud left by the receding flood waters in which crops could be grown, and *deshret* (red land), because in certain light the desert appears to glow red as a warning to any traveller.

65
Egypt

An Egyptian priest and historian called Manetho in the third century BC wrote a history of Egypt called *Aegyptiaca* and he is credited with dividing Egyptian history into dynasties. His writings have not survived intact

Above: A temple at Thebes built by Tuthmosis III showing a Christian icon painted on the second column early in the first century AD (see below)

Facing page: Ramesses II, thought by some to be the Pharaoh of the Exodus

but parts are quoted in other works. The Egyptian dynasties reach back well before the time of Abraham, and Egypt is a powerful force on the world stage throughout Old Testament history.

Thebes in the southern part of Egypt was a magnificent capital and many items in the Museum come from that area. It was once fabulously wealthy, until conquered by Assyria in 663 BC. Warning the Assyrian capital of her own coming destruction, the prophet Nahum has only to point back to the devastation of Thebes in 663 BC as an illustration of what awaits Nineveh (Nahum 3:8–10). Jeremiah and Ezekiel warn Thebes of judgement that will soon fall on her from Babylon (Jeremiah 46:25–26 and Ezekiel 30:13–19). The chief deity of Thebes was the god Amun.

Room 65 Egypt
As we enter this room we have stepped back one thousand years! Here you will experience the culture of Israel in Egypt over 400 years from the time of Joseph to Moses. Although much in this room is well before Moses, Egyptian culture would have changed little over the years.

In *case 1* on your right as you move to the opposite exit is a ***Cuneiform tablet from El-Amarna (WAA 29791)*** See also room 57 on page 44 This is a letter from Tushratta king of Mittani to Pharaoh Amenhotep III and contains a request for a gift as 'gold is as dust in the land of my brother.' This helps us to understand what riches Moses gave up when he left Egypt considering, 'disgrace for the sake of Christ as of greater value than the treasures in Egypt' (Hebrews 11:26).

Enter Room 64 and turn left. Notice the display on the ***Pyramids***. When first seen by European travellers they were mistakenly thought to be the store houses Joseph built (Genesis 41:48). Here is a fragment of the

Egyptian kings

A precise chronology for the dynasties of Egypt is not possible. As a rule of thumb, after 500 BC the dates are fairly accurate, from 500 to 1500 BC there is a margin of error of 20 years, and before 1500 BC the margin is at least 100 Years. We have listed only those Pharaohs associated with the Bible. For the chronology of Joseph see A timeline from Abraham to Solomon on page 23.

	BC	
Khety II	2115–2070	Abraham into Egypt about 2091BC (Genesis 12:10–20).
Amenemhat II	1922–1878	Joseph probably entered his service in 1885 (Genesis 41:41).
Sesostris II	1880–1874	Jacob settled in Egypt (Genesis 47:9).
Sesostris III	1874–1855	Joseph probably Prime Minister in his reign and Jacob died.
Amenemhet IV	1808–1799	Joseph died during his reign in 1806.
Tuthmosis III	1479–1425	The Pharaoh of the oppression and/or the Exodus (early date).
Amenophis (Amenhotep)II	1427–1400	Or the Pharaoh of the Exodus (early date). Part co-regency with Tuthmosis III.
Amenhotep III	1390–1352	See The Amarna Letters on page 44.
Amenhotep IV (Akhenaten)	1352–1336	See note on Egyptian king list on page 79.
Tutankhamun	1336–1327	Items from his tomb illustrate many biblical objects.
Ramesses II	1279–1213	Pharaoh of the Exodus (late date).
Siamun	978–959	Possibly the Pharaoh when Solomon sealed an alliance by marrying his daughter (1 Kings 3:1).
Shosheng I*	945–924	Shishak who sacked the temple in Jerusalem in 925 (1 Kings 14:25).
Taharqa*	690–664	The Tirhakah who threatened Sennacherib in 2 Kings 19:9.
Tantamani	664–656	Assyrian king Ashurbanipal sacked Thebes (Nahum 3:8–10).
Necho II*	610–595	Defeated Josiah and imprisoned Jehoahaz (2 Kings 23:29–35).
Apries*	589–570	The Hophra referred to in Jeremiah 44:30.
Augustus *	27– AD 14	Augustus was the first Roman Emperor to take the title of Pharaoh in Egypt. Joseph took Mary and the infant Jesus to Egypt (Matthew 2:13).
Arab conquest	AD 640	Muslim invaders reduced the Christian church.

* These kings are mentioned by name in the Bible

For list of Hebrew kings page 40. Babylonian kings page 50 Persian kings page 60. Assyrian kings page 84. Roman Emperors page 102

The date of the Exodus

Biblical scholars are divided between two alternative dates for the Exodus, these are 1446 BC ('early date') and 1220 BC ('late date').

The main evidence for the early date is based on 1 Kings 6:1. Solomon began the construction of the Temple in the fourth year of his reign which was 480 years after the Exodus. David's death and Solomon's succession to the throne is set around 970 BC. If this date is exact the Pharaoh of the Exodus was probably Tuthmosis III (1479–1425) or Amenophis II (1427–1400 BC).

The main evidence for the later date is the reference to the store cities of Pithom and Ramesses in Exodus 1:11; archaeological evidence would appear to locate the Exodus in the time of Ramesses II who reigned from 1279–1213 BC. A text of his time refers to slave labour called the *Hapiru*— perhaps the Egyptian word for the Hebrews—to build his grain cities. However, it could be that the Israelites in Exodus were building cities that were later rebuilt in the time of Ramesses. The chronology in this guide assumes the early date.

limestone casing block (EA 490) from the largest pyramid, built for Khufu (2551–2525 BC).

On the left in *case 1* at the far end of the room is *a reed basket (EA58695)*. Though much older than the time of Moses it recalls the history of Exodus 2. According to Exodus 2:3 that basket, unlike the one you are looking at, was waterproofed with 'tar and pitch'.

Rooms 63 and 62—the Roxie Walker Galleries—Egyptian burial and funeral rites contain *coffins and mummies.*

The book of Genesis closes with the words 'Joseph died… They embalmed him, and he was placed in a coffin in Egypt' (Genesis 50:26). Joseph, as a man of high rank, would have been

Above: A reed basket from Egypt dated around 4000BC (EA58695)

embalmed and mummified exactly as you see examples in these rooms. His body would have been placed in a great wooden coffin (or perhaps a stone one similar to those we will see later in Room 4) and we may wonder whether his coffin included the elaborate drawings and plans to direct the spirit of the deceased to the underworld or whether he had left instructions that such was unnecessary!

Above: A model of ploughing (EA41576) found in an Egyptian tomb

Much of our knowledge of Egyptian life comes from the little models that were included in the tombs of the great people in Egypt. In these next two rooms resist the temptation to spend all your time just looking at mummies and coffins and take particular note of the artefacts as they can teach us a lot about culture and customs.

In **Room 63** *case 5* there are examples of baking, brewing and butchery, and other household items that would have been familiar to Israel in Egypt. Look for the **head-rest** *(EA41579)*; this may appear uncomfortable, but it served the purpose of keeping the head (and therefore ears and hair) above the ground-crawling insects. Compare Jacob at Luz: 'Taking one of the stones there, he put it under his head and lay down to sleep' (Genesis 28:11).

Case 4 introduces us to *Life, death and rebirth.* This explains the Egyptian approach to death with reference to the major gods Osiris and Ra. Here is the large cedar coffin of Gua around 1850 BC *(EA30839)*—Joseph (Genesis 39–50) would therefore have been very familiar with coffins like this. The large eyes, always on the east

Above: The interior of the outer coffin of a chief physician c. 2000BC illustrating the two ways to the underworld. (EA30839)

side of coffins, enabled the deceased to look towards the rising sun; inside is a painted door to allow the spirit to go in and out on its journey. See Box: The Book of the Dead on page 73.

Notice in this case the painted wooden statuette of a female servant *(EA30716)* which helps to illustrate the history of the baker in the story of Joseph (Genesis 40:16).

The nearest mummy to the time of Joseph you will find in *case 8* the **mummy of Ankef** *(EA46631)*. It is dated *c* 1950 BC.

However, a more splendid display is *case 10* (in the centre to the right) **the coffin of King Intef** *(EA 6652* dated *c* 1600 BC. See picture on page 74.

Bulls, bricks and baubles

At the far end of **Room 63** on your right in *case 11* there is a **collection of food offerings**: pomegranates, loaves, cakes, dates and duck. See picture on page 17. Notice also the model granary *(EA2463)* and exhibits from the royal tombs in the Valley of the Kings, including those who may have been kings in the time of the Exodus.

As you enter **Room 62** turn to your left and *case 24* (half-way along). Notice the example of the **Book of the Dead**, *no.8* on the right (EA 9901/3).

At the far end of **Room 62** on the right in *case 28* notice the mummies of the **sacred bull** *(EA 6773)*. These are of later Roman date, but the practice was unchanged from the time of Israel in Egypt. The sacred Apis bull (herald of the god Ptah), Buchis bull (sacred to Ra and Osiris), and Mnevis bull (sacred to Ra at Heliopolis) were worshipped, and when they died were embalmed and buried. Another young bull—without blemish— had to be found to take its place. The plague recorded in Exodus 9:1–7 would have affected the current sacred bulls! It is the worship of the sacred bulls that lies behind the episode of the golden calf in Exodus 32. Centuries later the prophet Ezekiel reminded Israel that many of them had never left Egyptian worship behind them: 'Nor did they forsake the idols of Egypt' (Ezekiel 20:8).

In **Room 61 Egypt** immediately in front of you is *case 35*. To the right of it notice the model of the **offering by the king** before the Apis bull *(EA22920)*. See picture on page 75. Also here is a sistrum *(EA38172)*—this is a rattle used in worship and was considered by the Egyptians as sacred to the

Above: Female servant carrying a tray of cakes on her head (EA30716) *(Height: 34cm)*

Above: The Book of the Dead with Osiris weighing the heart against the feather of truth (EA 9901/3)

The Book of the Dead

There were several versions of the Book of the Dead (sometimes known as the Book of the Two Ways). Gaining access to the happy land 'located somewhere in the Far West', depended on leading a virtuous life on earth. The deceased had to pass through a series of ordeals: the ferry-man must be persuaded to take the dead across the River of Death, then came the twelve gates guarded by fearful serpents. Amulets and a copy of the Book of the Dead—with relevant spells and a map to work out how to pass the many dangers—were buried with the dead person. At the Lake of Fire, forty-two Assessors read out a list of sins and wrong doings and the deceased had to swear that he was innocent of them all. If that test was passed, he was admitted to the judgement hall of Osiris, where the heart was weighed against the feather of truth. Sometimes an inscribed scarab beetle (see page 45) has been found placed over the heart of a mummy with the words: 'My heart, do not testify against me at the judgement!' If the life had been full of sin, the scales would tip against the deceased and they would be fed to Ammut—the crocodile-headed monster. If the life had been virtuous, the deceased could join the ancestors in the kingdom of the West.

goddess Hathor. It was used in Egyptian temple rituals to purify the gods and ward off evil. See also 2 Samuel 6:5.

On the other side of *case 35* there is a large **Nile mud brick** *(EA6020)*—see picture on page 76. The chopped straw used to strengthen it is clearly visible; this brick has the official name of Ramesses II stamped on it. Some think this is the Pharaoh of the Exodus, but whether he is or not the brick would be similar to those made by the Israelites. (See Box: The date of the Exodus on page 70). They were engaged in building great store cities for Pharaoh (see Exodus 1:8–14) and the importance of straw in brick making is seen clearly from the history in Exodus 5:1–23.

Case 36 displays the beautiful jewellery of Egypt, and *case 37* the beauty treatments about the time of Moses.

Cases 38 and *39* are of interest in displaying Egyptian household items and entertainment.

The walls of this room (start from the left) illustrate the development of Egyptian writing.

Case 14 illustrates writing equipment, *case 15 no.4* shows how tightly a papyrus scroll could be rolled and *case 25 no.1* is a good example of writing on papyrus in the 2nd century AD at the time the New Testament was being copied in the same way.

Turn into **Room 59** and descend the West Stairs taking the first exit right into **Room 4— Egyptian sculpture**

Pharaohs of Egypt

The first thing you meet in **Room 4** is a large *granite scarab (EA 74)*. This is a dung beetle that we met in Room 19 (page 45).

Behind you to your left on the wall are two stele of the Roman emperors Tiberius (EA617) and Domitian *(EA709)*, both taking the title of Pharaoh of Egypt. Under Tiberius, Jesus Christ died: probably under Domitian, the

Above: A bronze statuette of an unnamed ruler worshipping an Apis bull, about 600 BC (EA22920). Length: 20cm

Facing page: Coffin of King Intef c.1600 BC within two hundred years of the time that Joseph was in Egypt (EA 6652)

apostle John was exiled to Patmos (Revelation 1:9). See list of Roman Emperors on page 102.

Further along on your left is a beautifully carved black rock **sarcophagus of Ankhnesneferibre (EA 32)**. An excellent example of Egyptian hieroglyphic writing; this princess was alive in the time of Jeremiah (in the sixth century BC) who warned of judgement on the Pharaoh: 'I am going to hand Pharaoh Hophra King of Egypt over to his enemies' (Jeremiah 44:30).

Notice further on your left in the middle the grey granite ram representing the god **Amun with King Taharqa (EA 1779)**–see picture on page 77. This is the 'Tirhakah king of Cush' in

2 Kings 19:9. Cush was south of Egypt in what we know as Nubia or northern Sudan. Tirhakah was the 'broken reed' that Hezekiah relied on as an ally when he was threatened by Sennacherib of Assyria (Isaiah 36:1–6).

The large bust in the centre of the room is that of **Ramesses II (EA19)**—see picture on page 66. He is considered by some to be the Pharaoh of the Exodus. See Box: The date of the Exodus on page 70. Notice the skilful workmanship that made use of a single block of coloured granite.

Cross the centre of the room and notice in the glass case on your right, between the two pillars:

Above: Nile mud brick from the time of Ramesses II (EA6020). Length: 38cm

Below: A necklace of gold, glass and coloured stones from the time of Moses (EA65617)

the *limestone dyad of man and wife* (EA36). This is a detailed example of Egyptian costume and head dress typical of the time of Moses.

Further down on the right is *Tuthmosis III (EA 61)* whose date could place him as the Pharaoh of the oppression (Exodus 1: 11–14); alternatively some believe that it is the statue of Amenophis II, who, under the early date could be Pharaoh of the plagues and Exodus (Exodus 14). See Box: The date of the Exodus on page 70.

Wing nuts and heresies

Continuing on the right are two statues of *Sesostris III (EA 684, 685)* who is sometimes playfully nicknamed 'wing nuts' because of his ears!

Almost at the end of Room 4 on the right is the *Rosetta Stone (EA 24)*. This highly significant discovery has an interesting indirect bearing on our Bible tour. See Box: The Rosetta Stone on page 78.

On the wall opposite the

Above: The god Amun in the form of a ram with Pharaoh Taharqa (EA1779). This Pharaoh was the 'broken reed' of Hezekiah's trust (Isaiah 36:6; 2 Kings 19: 9). The inscription in the plinth describes how Taharqa 'fully satisfies the heart of his father Amun.'

Left: Sesostris III 'wing nuts' (EA 685) who may have been the Pharaoh in whose time Joseph was Prime Minister

Above: The Rosetta Stone (EA 24) has been in The British Museum since 1802 and is important in helping scholars decipher ancient Egyptian writing. The bottom left corner has been cleaned to show the original condition

The Rosetta Stone

The Rosetta Stone was discovered by a French officer in 1799 in the western Delta of Egypt. It was surrendered to the British during the Napoleonic war and was brought to the British Museum in 1802. The stone is carved on black basalt and is valuable because it contains the same message in two forms of ancient Egyptian writing and one in Greek. The Egyptian writing at the top of the stone is hieroglyphic writing, whilst the second section is demotic Egyptian; the third section is in Greek capital letters (known as 'uncial'). See Box: A Short History of Writing on page 28. The Greek was translated relatively easily and proved to be part of a citation by Egyptian priests in Memphis to celebrate the first anniversary of the coronation of Ptolemy V in 196 BC. The two Egyptian scripts were found to be the equivalent text and, once deciphered, this helped scholars to understand ancient Egyptian writing. The hieroglyphic script would have been known to Israel during their time in Egypt; Moses, who was educated in the Royal Court of Pharaoh (see Acts 7:22) may have been accustomed to reading a script like this.

Above: Part of the Egyptian king list that deliberately ignored history that the Egyptians preferred to forget (EA117)

Rosetta Stone is an **Egyptian king list** *(EA117)* from the temple of Ramesses II at Abydos. This unimpressive block of hieroglyphics is interesting in that it omits four Egyptian kings. This was a deliberate omission because these kings, including Tutankhamun, were involved in what is known as the 'Amarna heresy'. Amenhotep IV (husband of the Egyptian beauty Nefertiti) changed the national religion from polytheism to the sole worship of the Sun god, the Aten; Amenhotep changed his name to Akhenaten (worshipper of Aten). Although Tutankhamun reinstated the old religion, ancient historians simply ignored unpalatable events. Therefore, do not expect the Egyptians to record the devastating plagues under the hand of Moses or the escape of so many slaves with the loss of imperial charioteers. Similarly the Assyrians would not record the widespread adoption of Israel's God after the preaching of the prophet Jonah (Jonah 3:5) or the defeat of Sennacherib's army outside Jerusalem (2 Kings 19:35).

Go to the Black Obelisk further down on the left in **Room 6.**

⑥ Fire from the North

Brilliant mathematicians, astronomers, engineers and warriors, yet the men from the land of Ashur struck fear and terror into many hearts. Lord Byron wrote, 'The Assyrian came down like a wolf on the fold' and to many these people were just a bunch of vicious thugs. Cruelty and fear were certainly weapons in the Assyrian military arsenal

Room 6 Ancient Near East. By entering Room 6 we now move from Egypt to another great power, Asyria.

The Assyrians are coming!

The land of the Assyrians was in upper Mesopotamia and it was at the height of its power during the 8th and 7th centuries BC—from Uzziah to Hezekiah kings of Judah. The Bible places the Assyrians as the descendants of Ashur, the second son of Shem and thus a grandson of Noah (Genesis 10:22). One of their chief cities was Nineveh where Ishtar, the goddess of sex and war, was their patron deity. Assyria was perhaps the most consistently powerful and most feared nation of all in the ancient world. Some of the best known names from the Assyrian Empire are found in the Bible, including Sargon and his son Sennacherib.

The significant item in this room is the *Black Obelisk* on the left.

Above: Shalmaneser III —King of Assyria who refers to both Ahab and Jehu in his own records (ANE 118884)

Facing page: Winged human headed bull—one of a pair guarding the palace of Sargon, King of Assyria, at Khorsabad (WA118873)

The Black Obelisk

Discovered in 1845 by Henry Layard, the black limestone commemorates the triumphs of the Assyrian king Shalmaneser III. Part of this victory obelisk describes his defeat of Ben-Hadad and Hazael of Damascus (see 2 Kings 8:7–15) and depicts rulers in national costume bringing tribute to the king. The second row down shows a kneeling figure in Israelite dress. This may be Jehu himself, the son of Omri. The inscription above reads, 'Tribute of Yaua, house of Humri: I received silver, gold, a golden bowl, a golden vase with a pointed bottom, golden tumblers, golden buckets, tin, a staff for a king, spears.' This may be Jehu himself, the son of Omri. Jehu was not the direct son of Omri, but was a usurper and the fourth in line from Omri (there is no distinct word for grandfather/grandson in Hebrew). From the ninth to the seventh centuries Assyrian records often called Israel, *mat-Humri*—'land of Omri', or *bit-Humri*—'house of Omri'. Behind the kneeling figure is a line of his servants carrying the items of tribute.

Jehu was known to be a furious charioteer (2 Kings 9:20) and a ruthless soldier who destroyed the line of Ahab, including the infamous Jezebel. Having killed both the kings of Israel and Judah he needed a strong ally, and Shalmaneser provided that. Shalmaneser's account on the obelisk does not mention a defeat of Israel, so Jehu was probably buying help. However, the narrative did not end there. In

Above: The Black Obelisk showing the nations bringing tribute to Shalmaneser III. This took place in Shalmaneser's 18th year which was 841BC (Height: 198cm)

Facing page: Detail of the Black Obelisk showing the Israelites bringing their tribute. The kneeling figure may well be that of Jehu himself (ANE118885)

order to make a friend of Shalmaneser, Jehu abandoned Hazael of Damascus (in Syria). Hazael is also mentioned, on the obelisk, but he had resisted the Assyrian king. For this treachery Jehu and Israel paid dearly in later years as 2 Kings 10:32 reveals.

We three kings of Orient are...
Behind the Black Obelisk are the stelae of three kings. The one on the left is ***Shalmaneser III (ANE 118884)***—see picture on page 81. This is the king of Assyria who, though not recorded by name in the Old Testament, mentions both Ahab and Jehu. The writing on this stela describes his military campaign in the west in 853 BC. He confronted and defeated an alliance of nations and he lists the strength of each army. The reverse side of the stela refers to 'Ahab the Israelite' and claims that Ahab's army had 2,000 chariots and 10,000 infantry. This battle, probably around 853 BC, is not

referred to in the Bible which at the time is largely concerned with the constant squabbles between Israel and Syria. Shalmaneser III also refers to Adad-idri of Damascus (Syria); this is the Ben-Hadad of 2 Kings 6:24 and 8:7—but he didn't last very long either!

Beside Shalmaneser III is his father, Ashurnasirpal II. The third king is Shalmaneser's son. (Note: do not confuse Shalmaneser III with the Shalmaneser referred to in 2 Kings 17:3 and 18:9 during the time of Ahaz and Hezekiah, kings of Judah—that one is Shalmaneser V).

Now pass between the two winged lions *(ANE 118801–2)* **in Room 6** with the big gates in front of you.

The lions were to protect the throne-room from evil spirits. Did you notice anything unusual about these lions? In addition to the fact that they have wings and human heads they also have five legs—all the better to expel evil spirits!

Assyrian kings

Assyrian kings ruled much of what we know as northern Iraq and Syria from 1300–1050 BC; they lost power in the face of Aramean tribes until about 925 BC. As they reasserted their rule, they came into conflict with the kings of Israel and Judah. Note that only the first Old Testament reference to each king is given.

	BC	
Tukulti-Ninurta II	890–884	The reigns of Asa and Baasha, kings of Judah and Israel.
Ashurnasirpal II	883–859	The time of Ahab King of Israel and Elijah the prophet.
Shalmaneser III	858–824	His records mention subduing Ahab and Jehu (see the Black Obelisk on page 82).
Shamsi-Adad V	823–811	The reigns of Joash and Jehu, kings of Judah and Israel.
Adad-nirari III	810–783	Probably the 'deliverer' in 2 Kings 13:5.
Shalmaneser IV	782–773	During the reigns of Amaziah and Jeroboam II.
Ashur-dan III	772–755	Probably king when Jonah went to Nineveh.
Ashur-nirari V	754–745	The reigns of Azariah and Menahem.
Tiglath-pileser III *	744–727	2 Kings 15:29 (also the Pul of v 19). His records name Menahem, Pekah and Hoshea of Israel, and Ahaz of Judah.
Shalmaneser V*	727–722	2 Kings 17:3–6.
Sargon II*	722–705	Isaiah 20:1
Sennacherib*	704–681	2 Kings 18:13 The siege of Jerusalem in 701 BC
Esarhaddon*	680–669	2 Kings 19:37
Ashurbanipal*	668–627	The Aramaic name Osnapper is used in some translations of Ezra 4:10. See pages 50 and 93.

End of Assyria with the fall of Nineveh to Babylon in 612.
* These kings are mentioned by name in the Bible
For list of Hebrew kings page 40. Babylonian kings page 50. Persian kings page 60. Egyptian kings page 69. Roman Emperors page 102.

Above: The gruesome detail of the bottom panel of the Balawat gates of Shalmaneser III (ANE 121651)

'But Jonah ran away'

The small statue of **Ashurnasirpal II** *(ANE 118871)* stands on a plinth in the centre.

Examine the bottom panel of the great bronze gates on your left in **Room 6** (or the reconstruction behind the statue) from the palace of his son Shalmaneser III. You will see the grisly portrayal of enemies being dismembered or viciously killed.

Walk through **Room 7 Ancient Near East**

The walls are decorated with the sculptures from the palace of Ashurnasirpal II. He was unbelievably cruel, and once boasted, 'I built a pillar over against the city gate, and I flayed all the chief men who had revolted, and I covered the pillar with their skins. Some I walled up within the pillar, some I impaled upon the pillar on stakes, and others I bound round the pillar; and I cut off the limbs of the officers who had rebelled. From some I cut off their hands and from others I cut off their noses, their ears, and their fingers, of many I put out the eyes. Their young men and maidens I burned in the fire. The rest of them I consumed with thirst in the desert of the Euphrates.' Though Jonah lived 100 years later, it is little wonder that he was reluctant to go to a city with kings like this in control (Jonah 1:3).

Tiglath the terrible

On the central columns of **Room 8** to your right are two carvings. The one on the right is *Tiglath-pileser III (WA118900)* and on the left is one of his arms-bearers. When Ahaz, king of Judah, was threatened by a coalition of Israel and Syria he sent tribute to Tiglath-pileser (sometimes called Pul) to rid him of his troublesome neighbours. Ahaz then corrupted the worship of the LORD by copying an impressive altar that he saw in Syria (2 Kings 16:1–20).

Assyrian records show that King Hoshea was Tiglath-pileser's puppet king in Israel. Shalmaneser V considered him to be a traitor because he stopped paying tribute and sought Egypt's support, so he attacked Samaria and deported many Israelites into Assyria. (See 2 Kings 15:29; 17:1–6). This policy of wholesale exile by the Assyrians contributed to the breakdown of cultural barriers and paved the way for the future spread of Greek culture and of Christianity.

Walk into **Room 8 Ancient Near East**. Turn left into **Room 23** and on your left are two massive **human-headed winged bulls** (*WA118808–9*) from Khorsabad; these are the guardians of the palace of King Sargon. See Box: Khorsabad, the home of Sargon on page 88, and picture on page 80.

Now let's see how these two great guardians were 'dug' out of the ground.

Blood and guts!

Turn back into **Room 8** and then **9, Ancient Near East**. Just before the entrance to Room 9, notice on the left-hand side a carving of a vulture carrying intestines (*WA 118907*). In older translations of the Bible, bowels is a term used to denote not only the physical organs of the abdomen, but also the seat of mercy and affection. This slab shows how all who resisted the Assyrians would be treated: without mercy or affection.

Room 9 depicts Nineveh in the time of Sargon and Sennacherib. Look at the detailed panels on the wall to the right showing how those ten-ton bulls were carved and then lifted upright (*WA 124823*). Slave labour, including prisoners from Palestine, was used for this. Some of the many stone reliefs from Nineveh in this room show the scorching effects of fire that illustrate well the words of the prophet who warned of the end of Nineveh (Nahum 3:15). This happened when the city was destroyed by a coalition of Medes and Babylonians in August 612 BC.

Return into **Room 23** to the start of **Room 10** and turn left

Look at the inscription from under the stomach of a human headed winged bull from Nineveh (*WA 118815*). This includes the most detailed surviving account of the tribute sent by Hezekiah, king of Judah, after the Assyrian campaign to Palestine in 701 BC.

Above: Sargon and his son Sennacherib kings of Assyria (ANE 118822)

Now walk past the human-headed winged bulls towards the stairs opposite leading down to the lower floor but stop at the head of the stairs.

Famous for one line

You are standing in front of the great king *Sargon II (ANE 118822)*. Sargon is facing one of his high officials or more probably his son the crown prince Sennacherib. For years it was presumed that a king by the name of Sargon never existed because the only reference to him came in Isaiah 20:1. In the year 721 BC Sargon became king of Assyria; he continued the siege of Samaria begun by his predecessor Shalmaneser V (2 Kings 17:5–6 and 18:9–11) and when the city was destroyed he took all the credit. Sargon was the ruler of a vast empire and with a great ancestry, but he is mentioned in just one line in the Bible—this is because the focus of the Bible is upon Israel and Judah.

Continue into Room 10 The Lachish Room

'Sennacherib King of the world'

The terrifying siege of Lachish
In 701 BC Sennacherib, the son of Sargon, laid seige to Jerusalem. This took place during the reign of King Hezekiah and is vividly retold in 2 Kings 18–19, 2 Chronicles 32, and Isaiah 36–37. In this room you have Sennacherib's record of the events.

When Austin Henry Layard discovered this stone relief in 1847 it generated great excitement in Victorian England because it was the first archaeological confirmation of an event in the Bible. Isaiah 36:1–2 informs us: 'Sennacherib, King of Assyria, attacked all the fortified cities of Judah and captured them. Then the king of Assyria sent his field commander with a large army from Lachish to King Hezekiah at Jerusalem'. Sennacherib destroyed scores of towns across Judah, but he was unable to enter Jerusalem. When he returned to his capital at Nineveh, it was the destruction of Lachish that adorned the walls of his victory room. See Box: The Taylor Prism on page 48.

There is an artist's impression of the siege of Lachish to the left of the opposite door. The artist shows only one outer wall,

Khorsabad, the home of Sargon

In 1843 Paul-Emile Botta, a French vice-consul and archaeologist in Mosul (northern Iraq), discovered at Khorsabad on the banks of the River Tigris, 12 kilometres (8.5 miles) to the northeast of Nineveh, a great palace guarded by huge **human-headed winged bulls** each weighing around ten tons and standing 4.8 metres high (15 feet). The walls were lined with great slabs of stone carved with pictures and cuneiform writing. Botta had discovered the palace of King Sargon who is now one of the best known Assyrian kings and who was one of the most powerful rulers in the ancient world. Of the many documents left behind by Sargon, several contain a reference to his defeat of Israel: 'In the first year of my reign I besieged and conquered Samaria… I led away captive 27,280 people who lived there.' Sargon's own documents confirm that he replaced them with people from other nations he had defeated (see 2 Kings 17:6,24), and these brought their own religions and practices with them (vs 29–33). From now on the people from Samaria (Israel, in the north) became a mixed race with a mixed religion—no wonder that 'the Jews had no dealings with the Samaritans' (John 4:9).

Above: A detail of the seige of Lachish with captives being led into exile (WA 124907). Notice the 'battering ram' at the top left

whereas excavations at Lachish reveal there were two and this is a reminder of the defence systems that Hezekiah put in place at Jerusalem when he knew Sennacherib was coming (2 Chronicles 32:5). For a vivid and terrifying account of a similar siege see 2 Kings 6:24–29.

Artillery and storm troopers

The battle for the strategic city of Lachish begins in the second panel on the wall facing you as you enter. The top of the panel shows grapes and figs on the trees indicating that the attack took place in late summer. Among the soldiers, different nationalities are represented, including some Israelites captured and forced into battle and Iranians with long skirts. Notice the ranks of archers,

with quivers stuffed with arrows, firing over the walls into the city; some kneel, protected by the tall leather shields of the javelin throwers. Behind them are the bearded artillerymen with long pointed helmets and wielding their slings as they keep up a barrage of small but lethal missiles. Others are scaling the walls, firing arrows for a protective shield as they advance. For a description of this see Joel 2:1–9 where the picture of a swarm of locusts represents soldiers scaling a city wall. The air is thick with missiles. The siege-engines trundle up the earth and stone ramps to the walls of the city. Remains of the great ramp are still visible today. See picture on page 90. Each engine encloses an archer, a man to guide the 'tank',

Top: The siege ramp built by Sennacherib's army at Lachish is still visible today

Facing page: 'Sennacherib, King of the world'—the end of the siege of Lachish (WA 124911)

Facing page below: Prisoners playing their lyres—reminiscent of Psalm 137 (WA 124947)

and a 'fireman' who, with great ladles of water, douses the constantly falling fire-torches of the defenders as they try to set fire to the protective leather covering of the battering ram .

Desperate defence

For their part, the defenders are desperately hurling their fire-bombs and rocks upon the attackers; some soldiers are falling over the wall, victims of advancing archers. At the bottom of the panel is the gruesome scene of those who tried to escape the city and have been impaled on long stakes in the sight of the defenders. Groups of men and women, with children clinging to their mothers, are led away into exile taking their possessions with

them on camels and in heavily laden ox carts. This is the only picture of Judeans at this time available to us. The leaders of the city are spread-eagled and flayed alive, whilst others are summarily executed.

The great king loses face!

Sennacherib himself took part in this siege and he is seen receiving the defeated prisoners as he sits upon his high throne. The inscription reads, 'Sennacherib King of the world, King of Assyria, he sat on a throne and the booty of Lachish passed before him.' The king's chariot and bodyguard are below and behind him. Notice how the king's face has been hacked out—perhaps the vengeful work of a Babylonian

soldier when Nineveh itself was destroyed in 612 BC!

As you follow the relief round you will notice the picture of the base camp with priests offering sacrifices to their gods and the servants busy in their tents. This is the end of the Lachish sequence. The remaining panels depict Assyrian cavalry, slingers and archers, and prisoners being led

away under the watchful and taunting eye of the Assyrian guards. Some prisoners are playing their lyres, which is reminiscent of Psalm 137.

Before you leave this room notice the glass case containing items found at Lachish. The octagonal prism describes Sennacherib's campaigns, including Lachish. This is not the Taylor Prism (see page 48), nor was it found at Lachish. Notice the stones for slings that are reminiscent of David's battle with Goliath at an earlier period (1 Samuel 17:48–49).

Exit from **Room 10** via the way you came in and walk between the winged bulls.

Before you leave the great guardians of the palace look at the base of the one on the left. Recently discovered squares scratched on it show that guards, or those waiting for an audience with the King, may have been playing the *Royal Game of Ur* that we first met in Room 56 (page 30).

Ashurbanipal tells that his grandfather, Sennacherib, was assassinated between 'two colossi'—so, at Nineveh two great bulls like these witnessed the murder of Hezekiah's enemy. See 2 Kings 19:37.

Take the stairs beside the large relief of Sargon down to **Room 88** In order to keep the Assyrians in our mind, walk straight through this first part of **Room 88** and on the other side of the wall facing you is a display of weapons that the Assyrians used; here also is a saw of the kind that was used to carve the great human-headed bulls from the rock *(WA 121202)*.

Turn to your right and in the case in front of you is a clay tablet *(WAK 3751)* which contains part of the annals of Tiglath-pileser III; it mentions his campaigns against the kings of Judah, Ammon, Moab, Ashkelon, Edom, Gaza, and Tyre. (See 2 Kings 15:29).

'Mene, mene, tekel, parsin'

Further along is a case with many values of Mina weights in the shape of Lions *(WA 91220 on)*; The word 'mene' is similar to the Aramaic word for 'numbered' and mina was the name given to a weight (about 500 gm) as seen here. The Aramaic handwriting that appeared on the wall during

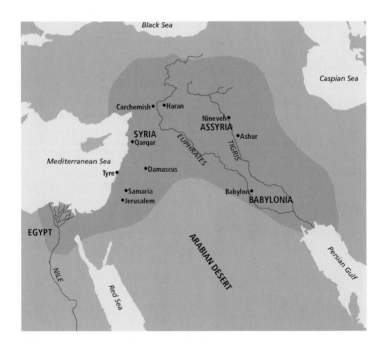

The Asyrian empire in the time Hezekiah

Above: The grisly banquet of Ashurbanipal and his queen with the head of his enemy hanging in a tree (WA 124920)

Below: The Aramaic word for 'numbered' is mene and the 'mina' weights reflect Daniel 5:25 (WA91220) Length: 25cm

the feast of Belshazzar read: 'Mene, mene, tekel, parsin' (Daniel 5:25). Daniel explained this as spelling the end of the king; he had been weighed and his days were numbered. We will find these weights again in Room 68 case 2 page 104

Also in this case are clay model dogs which were buried under doorways with magic spells to keep out intruders. One is inscribed: 'Don't think, bite'! *(no. 5)*. In the next display case are items of domestic use, including a bath.

Now walk into **Room 89** and go to the foot of the stairs opposite. You can start at

Episode 1 and follow round on this wall the campaign of the last great king of Assyria, Ashurbanipal; see Ezra 4:10 and also page 50. This stone relief graphically illustrates the barbarity of warfare in ancient times, and it culminates in a feast in the king's garden with a grisly trophy—the head of his defeated enemy—hanging in a tree *(WA 124920)*. Notice that, as with the face of Sennacherib in the Lachish room, the face of the king and queen here have been battered, presumably by an avenging Babylonian soldier in August 612 BC.

Urns of wonder

Return to the first part of **Room 88** where you entered. Immediately at the foot of the stairs you will see an urn and above it a leather scroll. This is a facsimile of one of the **Dead Sea Scrolls** which is a commentary on Habakkuk. Discovered in 1947, the Dead Sea Scrolls belonged to a religious community that had hidden their manuscripts from the Romans during the second century BC. Most of the books of the Old Testament are represented among the scrolls discovered, including a complete copy of Isaiah. Whereas the earliest Hebrew copy of Isaiah available had been dated around AD 900 (or 1600 years from the prophet himself), the Dead Sea Scrolls were dated approximately a century before Christ and therefore provided a much older copy—it confirmed the great accuracy of the texts of Isaiah.

To the right is a model of Herodium, near Bethlehem, where King Herod was buried, and beside this is the huge base of a column (WA 136209) from the palace of the Persian King Xerxes (Ahasuerus in the account of Esther)—see pages 60–61.

The rose-red city of Petra

In front of you is a reference to **Petra** the famous rose-red city. See No. 16 in the case. The Old Testament book of Obadiah describes this city in the rocks (Obadiah 3–4) that considered itself impregnable. The mother of Herod the Great was an Arab from the powerful Nabatean kingdom, whose capital was Petra. One of their last kings, Aretas, is mentioned in 2 Corinthians 11:32.

On to Jerusalem

Behind you is a model of the **Temple in Jerusalem** (WA 1997), as built by Herod the Great. Herod is considered by many archaeologists to be the greatest builder in Jewish history, surpassing even King Solomon.

Left: The rose-red city of Petra carved out of the sandstone. The Nabateans centred their kingdom at Petra

Facing page: Caves around the Dead Sea where the Qumran Scrolls were found

Note that one of the towers on the Antonia fortress is higher than the others; from here the Romans were able to keep a close watch on the Jews in their temple court (see Acts 21:30–32).

Beside this model you will find a *Babylonian astronomical almanac for 7/6BC (WA35429);* this is often referred to as the 'Star of Bethlehem' tablet because it records a star that some consider may be the one that is referred to at the nativity of the Christ child (Matthew 2:2).

A fascinating link with the New Testament is seen in the Ossuary *(WA126395)* to the right of the

Temple model. It has dual inscriptions in Hebrew and Greek. The Hebrew says that the occupant is 'Nicanor Alexa,' and the Greek reads 'Nicanor the Alexandrian'. A Nicanor of Alexandria presented a pair of bronze gates to the Temple in Jerusalem, which were famous for their beauty. The design on the side of the box may represent the design of those gates, and they were ones that Jesus and his disciples would have seen at the Temple.

Ascend the stairs and walk through **Room 10** into **Room 23**.

⑦ People of the way

A new development dramatically changed history when Jesus of Nazareth was executed. Historically, culturally, politically and spiritually the time was right for the spread of Christianity. A great deal of action is crammed into a small space, for the New Testament covers a period of less than a century compared with at least 3500 years of Old Testament history

From **Room 23 walk through Room 17 into Room 18** The Parthenon Galleries

Paul and the Parthenon!

The significance of The Elgin Marbles for our purpose is that the apostle Paul would certainly have seen these sculptures high up on the magnificent Parthenon when he visited the city around the year AD 50, a visit that is recorded in Acts 17. See Box: The Elgin Marbles on page 100.

> Return to **Room 23**, turn left up the short flight of stairs into **Room 22 Greece and Rome**

Diana—hunter and Amazons

Of interest at the far end of this room is the huge base of one of the columns of the *Temple of Diana in Ephesus* (GR1872.8–3.9). This is virtually all that is left of the original thirty-six sculptured columns, and the apostle Paul would have seen them all. In this city, Paul's preaching threatened the business of the craftsmen who made small household idols of Diana (see the picture on page 100); the riot that followed is recorded in Acts 19:21–41. See Box: Diana of the Ephesians on page 98.

Alexander the goat

On the wall to your right as you face the column is the bust of *Alexander the Great* (GR1872.5–15.1), the Macedonian who, between 334 and 323 BC, set out to conquer the world until the world ran out. Master of a million square miles of territory his military genius is legendary. He was depicted in Egypt as Pharaoh with ram's horns representing the god Amun. (See picture of Amun on page 77). Alexander was often referred to as 'the two-horned one'—a sign of deity, strength and

Facing page: Part of The Parthenon frieze depicting the Parthenon festival that commemorated the birthday of Athena, the Greek goddess. (South Frieze X, 26)

virility. The book of Daniel used the figure of a goat to represent him (Daniel 8:3–8).

Continue through **Rooms 23, 22, 21** and go down the stairs on the right into **Room 77—Greek and Roman architecture.** This section is subject to restricted opening, so check times on the 'Gallery availability' list. This room contains more of the 'archaic' and the 'modern' temple of Diana.(See Box below). At the far end is a base and lower drum from a column of the temple that Paul would have been familiar with (it is described as the 'fourth century' temple). On the left is a description of the temple and carved marble from it.

Turn into **Room 78—Classical inscriptions** in the far right-hand corner.

Above: Column base of the temple of Diana (GR 1872.8–3.9)

'Great is Diana of the Ephesians'

Diana is the Latin name of the goddess known in Greek mythology as Artemis. She was the daughter of Zeus and Leto, and elder sister of Apollo. She was the patroness of childbirth and the Amazons—a tribe of women who lived apart from men—and protectress of little children and all suckling animals. Artemis remained a perpetual virgin, though she symbolised fertility!

Revered as the moon goddess, she was a great hunter and often she is portrayed with packs of hunting dogs around her. At Ephesus Artemis was worshipped as a Nymph, and legend told that her image fell from the sky at Ephesus and that a shrine was built around it, and eventually a temple was erected around this. The Ephesians were proud of their role as guardians of the image of Artemis (Acts 19:35), and she became the centre of a lucrative tourist industry. Inscriptions confirm that

she was well known as 'Artemis the Great' (Acts 19:28). The first temple of Diana (referred to in the Museum as the 'archaic' temple), was built between 560 and 540 BC. It burned down in 356 BC and the building of a new temple began at once and lasted for 120 years. The temple roof was supported by 100 massive columns, 36 of which were sculptured. The temple became one of the seven wonders of the ancient world. It was finally destroyed by the Goths in AD 263.

Above: The Politarch Inscription reveals the careful accuracy of Luke as a historian (GR1877.5–11.1)

Clinical analysis

The Politarch Inscription (*GR1877.5–11.1*), confirms the accuracy of Luke (the compiler of *The Gospel of Luke* and *The Acts of the Apostles*) as a careful historian.

The Politarch Inscription is part of a Roman gateway discovered at Thessalonica and dated to the 2nd century AD. Its significance is that at Thessalonica the reference to the 'politarchs' or 'city officials' (Acts 17:6) is well attested by inscriptions from that town and it is known that the city had five politarchs in the first century. The first word in this inscription is written in Greek uncial (capital letters) and is from the verb *politarcheo*, 'to act as a politarch'. Four of the men listed in this inscription as politarchs bear the same names as men recorded in the New Testament: Sosipatros and Lucius (line 1 and 2

and see Romans 16:21) and Secundus (line 2 and see Acts 20:4) and Gaius (line 5 and see Acts 20:4). They are not the same men of course, but it shows that the names were common at that time.

Luke was a physician by profession and was well acquainted with the political arrangements in the various provinces of Asia; his correct use of titles for the local dignitaries reveals a clinical precision. Here are just a few examples: at the time Paul was in Cyprus a proconsul was in charge, and Luke used exactly the correct title when referring to Sergius Paulus (Acts 13:7). Philippi was accurately described as a Roman colony whose officials are referred to as *stratagoi* or magistrates (16:38). In Ephesus the 'officials of the province' are called the *Asiarchs* (19:31), exactly the people we now know controlled religious affairs there. At Malta the *protos* (28:7) is the 'chief official'. Small things? Perhaps, but these are details that would not be known to later generations and are therefore evidence that Luke was an eyewitness of all that he recorded.

On the opposite wall in the centre are tombstones from Ephesus, one from the time of Claudius in AD 54 (1867.11–22.415)—perhaps within months of Paul's visit to the city (Acts 19), and below it is an inscription written in both Latin and Greek which is reminiscent of John 19:20 (1867.11–22.416).

Retrace your route up the West Stairs to **Room 59**. Turn right into **Room 73** and continue through to **Room 70— Greece and Rome**. Immediately on the left on case 1 is a bust of Augustus (GR1911.9–1.1).

Nero 'the mad butcher of Rome'

In *case 3* there is an interesting collection of *coins from the time of Nero*. In order to create a brown-field site for urban redevelopment and the construction of his Golden House, Nero was probably responsible for the great fire of Rome in AD 64 and this may have led directly to the martyrdom of both Peter and Paul in the same year. Some of these coins were minted in the year of the fire. Beside this collection are *wall paintings* from Nero's 'Golden House' that he built after the fire.

As you continue notice the busts of many Roman emperors on your left: *Augustus*—the

The Elgin Marbles—sculptures from the Parthenon

The Parthenon, the central focus on the Acropolis in Athens, was built between 447 and 438 BC and was dedicated to Athena, the goddess and patroness of the city—nearly 500 years before Paul arrived there. A thousand years after its construction, the building was converted to be used as a Christian church, and it was finally ruined in 1687 by an explosion—the Turks had used the Parthenon as a store for their gunpowder! From the ruins, Lord Elgin brought these sculptures to England and they came into the possession of the British Museum in 1816. Many of the sculptures you see here depict scenes from mythology, but the procession that makes up the frieze, illustrates the impressive Panathenaic festival commemorating the birthday of Athena. The frieze well illustrates how devoted the Athenians were to their deities (see Acts 17:22).

Emperor at the time of the birth of Christ (*GR1879.7–12.9*)—and his wife *Livia*. Also the Emperors *Tiberius* (GR 1812.6–15.2)—the Emperor at the time of the Crucifixion of Christ (*GR1812.6–15.2*).

To the left in *case 14* there is an excellent collection of first century **oil lamps**. Lamps have a long history, and the basic open bowl with a groove for the wick changed little over the millennia. By the Greek period, moulds were made to produce lamps for the mass market, and the Romans decorated their moulds. Christian symbols were being added by the third century AD and some are exhibited here (see page 103). Because of its widespread domestic use, the lamp also became a symbol of spiritual light and life (Matthew 5:15 and John 1:7; 5:35 for example). The multiple lamps would be owned by wealthy families.

Titus—who was responsible for the destruction of Jerusalem in AD 70 (*GR 1909.6–10.1*).

Notice on the right as you leave this room *Septimus Severus*

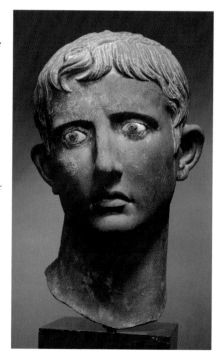

Above: An oil lamp of the type commonly in use in the time of Jesus Christ. Sessame oil would be poured into the reservoir and a wick of flax placed in the end; such lamps were placed on a stand or in a niche in the wall. From a private collection. Length: 12cm

Right: Augustus was the Roman Emperor at the time of the birth of Jesus. This bust is in Room 70 as you enter (GR 1911.9–1.1) Height: 43cm

Facing page: Bronze statuette of Artemis (Diana) possibly from Ephesus itself: 2nd–1st century BC (GR 1951.6-6.14)

Roman Emperors

	AD	
Augustus*	27 BC– AD 14	Birth of Jesus Christ.
Tiberius*	14–37	Life, death and resurrection of Jesus Christ.
Gaius (Caligula)	37–41	The conversion of Paul and the formation of the church.
Claudius*	41–54	Acts 11:28 and 18:2.
Nero	54–68	Persecution of Christians, martyrdom of Peter and Paul. Some of Nero's household converted (Philippians 4:22).
Vespasian	69–79	Jerusalem destroyed in AD 70 by his son Titus.
Titus	79–81	Eruption of Vesuvius and Colosseum built.
Domitian	81–96	Possibly in his reign John was exiled on Patmos.
Hadrian	117–138	Hadrian's Wall built in the north of England.
Septimus Severus	193–211	Severe persecution of Christians.
Diocletian	284–305	From this period there were often two and sometimes more rival emperors.
Constantine the Great	306–337	Christianity becomes the official religion of the empire. In AD 330 Constantine moved his capital from Rome to Byzantium, which he renamed Constantinople, and this marks the commencement of the Byzantine empire and culture which lasted until the fall of the city to the Turks in 1453.
Magnentius	350–353	The chi-rho emblem on his coins.

* These kings are mentioned by name in the Bible
For list of Hebrew kings page 40. Babylonian kings page 50. Persian kings page 60. Egyptian kings page 69. Assyrian kings page 84.

Right: Bust of Septimus Severus—in the Victorian Entrance Hall—who was responsible for severe persecution of Christians in the Roman Empire (GR1805.7–3.104)

Left: Part of a plaque depicting a gladiator fighting lions (GR1866.4–12.13)

Below: A reproduction of the armour of a 1st century Roman centurion—a familiar sight to Jesus and his disciples

(GR1802.7–10.2) who was responsible for severe persecution of the Christians.

Continue into **Room 69 Greece and Rome: daily life.** This provides an excellent introduction to first century AD. Notice the display *case 20* depicting the gladiator contests. In the second century BC one public contest lasted for 117 days and involved nearly 5,000 pairs of gladiators. Women were included and Christians became part of the entertainment as they were turned over to wild animals. The barbaric 'sport' was abolished in AD 400 largely through Christian influence. It is worth browsing in this room to get a feel for first-century life. In *case 26* on the left wall notice two moulds for making lamps with the Christian chi-rho motif (GR1975.1–29.1). These are dated in the fourth or fifth centuries AD and were made in Tunisia though they come from Rome. In *case 6* notice the small onyx scent bottle (GR1869.2–5.6) and compare with the picture of an alabaster bottle on page 104. This recalls the account in Matthew 26:6–13 where the word *alabastron* refers to a small bottle like these, rather than a box or a jar.

In *case 32* at the far end, there is a small bronze figurine of Artemis (Diana) of the Ephesians (Acts 19) (GR1951.6–6.14); the accumulation of gods in this case reminds us of Paul in Athens (Acts 17). See Box: The Elgin Marbles on page 100 and see also page 97.

At the end of **Room 69** turn left into **Room 68 Money.**

Money for all reasons

Fascinating though this whole gallery is, we are concerned only with those exhibits that relate to the Bible. On the right hand side at the far end in *case 1* **Valued Materials as Money** you can see how money began. Long before coins were used, metal would represent the value of items. *No. 1* is a clay tablet from Mesopotamia (1750 BC) tabling the value of ploughing oxen, and *section 4* **The coming of coinage** presents a time line of the development of coins.

In *case 2 panel 1 no. 2*, you will find a **royal mina** (WA 97188) from the time of Shalmaneser V (2 Kings 17: 3–6 and see page 86). See Room 88 pages 92–93 for the mina.

In *case 2 panel 4* **Authority and Organization** notice the coin from Ephesus in the 3rd century AD (*no. 26*). This is in the time of the Roman Emperor Maximus (AD 235–238)

and his image would be stamped on one side; however, on the reverse side the local city could choose their own image and the Ephesians inevitably chose the Temple of Artemis (Diana)—see page 98. This is the temple the apostle Paul was familiar with.

Now cross to *case 5*. In *panel 2* **The Market Place** you will gain some idea of the value of coins in the time of the Roman Emperor Titus—the apostle John was still alive at this time. Two brass *sestertii* (*nos 1,2*) would purchase three pounds of bacon and a pound of lard. Two copper *asses* (*nos 3,4*) in the time of Domitian are shown here. These two would buy you 100 hobnails for your boots—the nails are shown alongside (*no. 5*). But you would need 48 to buy a tunic. *No. 6* is *a quadrans* from the time of Domitian and that would purchase 3 pints of beer.

Case 5 panel 4 *no. 28* a coin of the emperor Caracalla (AD 186–217) a cruel and extravagant Emperor who was finally

Above: An alabastron used for storing perfume or ointment. The top was sealed with mud or clay and the neck of the jar pinched so that it could be broken to pour out the contents. This example from Palestine in the time of Christ is from a private collection. Height: 10cm

Top: A shekel from Tyre

Below: A denarius or 'Tribute Penny' referred to in Matthew 22:19

assassinated. This coin was minted in the Greek city of Cyzicus (now Belkis in northwest Turkey) somewhere between AD 198 and 217. Look carefully behind the head of the Emperor and you will see the Christian monogram chi-rho scratched there. Was this an act of defiance or witness in a severe time of persecution? The bust of the Emperor is not defaced as that would be an act of treason.

Case 3 panel 2 **Creating a Money Supply** introduces us to a bronze coin *(no. 14)* of Emperor Nero under whom both Peter and Paul were martyred for their Christian faith, and the gold coin *(no. 28)* of Augustus, in whose reign Jesus Christ was born, is inscribed with the words: 'for mending roads'.

Case 3 panel 3 **Money to Make Money** displays a denarius *(nos 20–21)* from the time of Tiberius. This is known as the 'Tribute Penny' and is referred to in the question and answer recorded in Matthew 22:19 between Christ and the Pharisees. According to Matthew 20:2 the same coin could be used for a labourer's daily wage. Since Tiberius was Emperor for most of Christ's adult life, it would probably have been a coin

Above: Coin of Constantine, the first Roman Emperor to embrace Christianity

just like this that was shown to him.

Nos 22,23 are 1st century silver shekels from Tyre. The shekel is not referred to in the New Testament, but the *didrachmon* of Matthew 17:24—the Temple tax—was equivalent to half a shekel hence some translations refer to it as the 'half shekel tax'. This was paid annually by every Jewish man, and the Temple authorities insisted on payment in coins from Tyre since these were of higher quality silver. The coin Peter found in the mouth of the fish was possibly from Tyre and thus was sufficient for both him and Jesus.

Panel 4 **Money with a Message. In** the absence of bill-boards and the media, it was soon realised that coins could be a valuable tool for propaganda.

No. 1 is a coin of the **Jewish King Antigonus** with the seven-branched candle stand (the *menorah*) on it. *Nos 2, 3* depict the **Emperors Caligula and Augustus**

in the attitude of worship.

No. 12 is of the **Emperor Constantine I** with his faced raised towards heaven; he was the first Roman Emperor to embrace the Christian faith. See Box: The Emperor and the Cross on page 110. Coins of Constantine and his sons are still often discovered in Britain today.

No. 13 is a coin of **Magnentius** (AD 350–353) and is significant because this is possibly the earliest use of the Christian monogram chi-rho officially stamped on a coin. For early Christian symbols see page 112–113.

No. 14 is from the short rule of **Olybrius** (AD 472) and the coin bears a cross and Latin words *salus mundi*—salvation of the world.

By the time of **Theodosius II** (AD 402–450) the cross has become a regular feature on the emperor's coins *(No. 15)*.

During the **Jewish uprisings** in AD 66–70 and again in AD 132–135 the Jews minted coins

Above: Coin of Magentius (AD 350–353). Possibly the earliest use of the Christian monogram chi-rho officially stamped on a coin

Right: Coin of Caracalla with a Christian emblem scratched onto it

with Hebrew inscriptions and symbols on them *(nos 31–34)*, and they even over-stamped Roman coins to express their rebellion *(no. 35)*.

The **Emperor Titus** (AD 79–81) retaliated by producing coins to celebrate the defeat and destruction of Jerusalem and its temple in AD 70 *(nos 36,37)*.

Nero—'the mad butcher of Rome'—used coins for his own propaganda *(nos 38–41)*.

If we turn the clock back a little, it is interesting to note that **Julius Caesar** was the first Roman

to appear on coins in his lifetime, and this silver denarius *(no. 52)* was minted in 44 BC. The silver denarius *(no. 53)* was minted for **Brutus** (43/42 BC) to justify the murder of Caesar.

Finally in this case, there is a gold aureus from the reign of **Augustus** (no. 54) and from now on the image of the emperor on coins became a standard practice. Thus the response of Jesus in Matthew 22:19 is of interest since it was a fairly recent innovation.

8 Christianity comes to Britain

Far from the centre of Roman power was an inhospitable and wild island. Yet this outpost of the empire received Christianity, but how did it come to these shores and what effect did it have on the lives of the ordinary people? It was here at York that the first Roman emperor to embrace the Christian faith was hailed as Augustus

Continue into **Rooms 37, 36,** down the corridor into **Room 41— Europe**

Pause at the **marble sarcophagus** (M&LA1957 10–11.1) just as you enter the room. This was made from marble quarried in Asia

41 Europe

Minor (Turkey) towards the end of the 3rd century AD, and clearly was commissioned by an adherent to the Christian faith because the carvings tell the narrative of Jonah—a symbol of death and resurrection. Immediately behind you in case 9, notice the coins of Constantine (see Box: The Emperor and the Cross on page 110), and others of that period including his mother, Helena (no. 3), and his 'Christian standard'—the Labarum (no.13).

In this room there are many interesting objects with Christian motifs from the early Byzantine period (see note on pages 102 and 110)—but this is beyond our present tour.

Continue by turning left into **Room 49— Roman Britain**

Rule Britannia!

The Romans came to Britain half a century before Jesus Christ was born. They never subdued the whole of 'Britannia'— as they called the island— and that is why the Emperor Hadrian began his wall in AD 122 from Tyneside to Solway—a distance of just over 117 kilometres (73 miles)—to keep out the troublesome Picts and Scots in the north. By and large however, the newcomers integrated well with the local inhabitants and trade and intermarriage were established and the population of Britannia soon rose to around two million. The coveted Roman citizenship was a route to

49 Roman Britain

Facing page: The 4th century mosaic from Hinton St Mary, Dorset. The central figure of Christ is surrounded in the four corners by what may be the four evangelists

influence and wealth and the 4th century saw the expansion of the great Roman villas. The remains of many villas and military encampments have been discovered, and we confidently expect more archaeological finds in the future.

The Romans have landed

At first the Roman pantheon of gods intermingled with Celtic mythology and the paganism of the natives. Just when Christianity first arrived in Britain is not known for certain. Almost certainly it came with merchants and Roman legionaries. But what evidence is there for the early arrival of Christianity?

Tertullian, the bishop of Carthage in North Africa, who died in AD 222, could boast that 'parts of Britain inaccessible to the Romans were indeed conquered by Christ'—though he does not specify which parts. What is certain is that by the Council of Arles in August 314, five representatives of the church in Britain attended—including the bishops of York, Lincoln and London. The significance of this Council was that it was called and

The Emperor and the Cross

There is an interesting story behind the chi-rho monogram (see page 113 for its meaning). In July 306 Constantine, whilst serving in Britain, was proclaimed Emperor at York. The following account was told by Constantine himself to Eusebius, an early Christian historian: In the year AD 312 Constantine was preparing for a battle with his rival Maxentius, when he saw a cross of light in the sky and the words 'In this sign conquer'. The following night he claimed that Christ appeared to him and commanded him to make a copy of what he had seen and use it as his standard. The result was his *Labarum* (pictured below on a coin of his realm; see also room 41 case 9 no. 13)—a tall pole with a cross-bar plated with gold; near the top was a wreath in gold and precious stones enclosing the chi-rho monogram. From the cross-bar hung a banner with his own portrait on it. From now on this always accompanied him in battle. The same monogram he ordered to be painted on the shields of his soldiers. Whatever the reality of his 'conversion' at this time, it is a fact that Constantine later embraced the Christian faith, ended the persecution of Christians, won all the battles he fought and became the sole Emperor of the Roman Empire. In AD 328 he enlarged the Greek city of Byzantium and renamed it Constantinople (modern Istanbul) making it the centre of Roman government above Rome itself. Probably Constantine was the first to use the chi-rho symbol officially— though we have seen it scratched on a coin possibly a century earlier in the time of Caracalla (see page 107).

Above and below: Hadrian's wall was completed in AD 126 and, according to Hadrian's biographer, was intended 'to separate the Romans from the Barbarians'.

presided over by the Roman Emperor, Constantine. See Box: The Emperor and the Cross, facing page. Only ten years earlier Diocletian had begun a bitter persecution of Christians throughout the empire.

It is therefore certain that the message of Jesus Christ was here long before Patrick (a Welshman) preached to the Irish in the 5th century, or Columba (an Irishman) preached to the Scots a century later; and it was certainly well established before Illtud was preaching to the Welsh or Augustine and Aidan to the English in the 5th, 6th and 7th centuries. But there is other firm evidence for this, and it lies in the discoveries you will find in this room.

By the end of the 4th century

the authority of Rome in Britannia had virtually run its course. With Rome's borders being squeezed throughout her empire, a weakened leadership, and a steady withdrawal of her armies, it was time to abandon this less than attractive outpost. When the Romans left, life became more insecure. The decay of Roman law and order, and increasing raids by fierce warriors from across the North Sea—the Anglo-Saxons—led many families to hide their treasures in the hope of returning to it in better days. They never did return, and it was what some of these families left behind that is so valuable for us.

Early Christian symbols

For the first three hundred years of Christianity, bitter persecution was experienced by those who followed 'the way' (Acts 9:2; 19:9,23), and they developed symbols that would help to identify the faithful.

The earliest Christian symbol was not the cross—which for the Romans represented the cruel death of a degraded criminal—but the first and last letters of the Greek alphabet, *alpha* and *omega*, which were often used to refer to Christ as the beginning and the end. This was prompted by Revelation 22:13 in the New Testament: 'I am the alpha and the omega, the first and the last, the beginning and the end.'

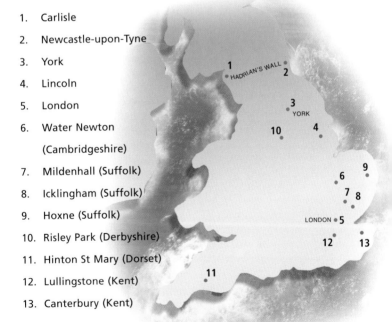

1. Carlisle
2. Newcastle-upon-Tyne
3. York
4. Lincoln
5. London
6. Water Newton (Cambridgeshire)
7. Mildenhall (Suffolk)
8. Icklingham (Suffolk)
9. Hoxne (Suffolk)
10. Risley Park (Derbyshire)
11. Hinton St Mary (Dorset)
12. Lullingstone (Kent)
13. Canterbury (Kent)

Map of England showing where the hoards of treasure were found

Above: A fourth century lead tank from Suffolk with the Christian chi-rho and the alpha and omega symbols (P&EE1946 2–4.1)

Here is alpha and omega in Greek capitals (known as uncials): ΑΩ (sometimes written as A W) and in lower case (though this minuscule script did not come into use until the seventh century AD) α ω

The early Christians also used the **symbol of a fish.** This was because the Greek word for 'fish' is *ichthus* (uncial: ΙΧΘΥΣ. minuscule: ιχθυς). The word forms an anagram for Jesus Christ God's Son Saviour:

I	Ιεσυς	Jesus
X	Χριστος	Christ
Θ	Θεου	God's
Y	Υιος	Son
Σ	Σωτηρ	Saviour

A fish was a very appropriate symbol for Christians—see for example Matthew 4:19; 13:37; 14:17.

However, the symbol that became most widespread was the **chi-rho** monogram which was made up from the first two letters of the name 'Christ'. In Greek the word 'Christ' today looks like this: Χριστος.

These three symbols are represented by some of the exhibits you will see in this room.

Immediately on entering **Room 49** look to your right and you will see a *lead tank (PRB 1946 2–4.1)* from an early Christian cemetery in Icklingham in Suffolk. Notice the chi-rho symbol with the omega placed before the alpha; perhaps the craftsman put the letters in the correct order in his mould so that the cast came out back to front; it is unlikely that he knew Greek but simply copied a drawing. The purpose of this tank is not known.

Left: Mildenhall silver spoon engraved with Christian symbols—a Roman legacy from the 4th century (PRB1946.10–7.27–34)

First, the tableware

Now for the treasures those families left behind under threat from the fierce Anglo-Saxons.

The Mildenhall treasure in case 22 (the cabinet on the left as you enter the room).

Some of this silverware is marked with the Christian chi-rho monogram and the alpha-omega letters.

In 1942, during the Second World War, a farmer, 'ploughing for victory' in his field in West Row, a small Suffolk hamlet near Mildenhall, turned up a hoard of buried treasure close by the remains of a 4th century Roman building. The thirty-four pieces of silverware were clearly 4th century in design and since the East Anglian coast was at the frontline of those Anglo-Saxon raids across the North Sea, it is very likely that the family valuables were hidden in haste. The fate of the family may be imagined. The Mildenhall Treasure was acquired by the British Museum in 1946.

Whilst much of the treasure is decorated with Bacchus, the god of wine, three of the spoons have in the centre of the bowl the chi-rho with the alpha and omega on either side of it (PRB1946.10–7.27–34).

Two other spoons have personal names: Papiltedo and Pascentia (husband and wife?) with *viva*—'may you live'—inscribed. According to inscriptions found with this set of tableware, they belonged to Eutherios, an influential minister under the emperor Julian (AD 360–363). Julian was a nephew of the Emperor Constantine and was brought up as a Christian, but

Above: *Part of the Hoxne treasure, silver ladles, some of which have the Christian chi-rho symbol engraved in the handle (PRBP.1994.4–8.42–61)*

when he became Emperor he revived pagan worship and was dubbed 'the apostate'.

In case 23 behind you, we have the **Hoxne Treasure** (Suffolk). Some of this also displays the chi-rho symbol. The Hoxne (pronounced 'Hoxon') Treasure was discovered in 1992 and was thought to have been buried at around the same time as the Mildenhall Treasure. It included 15,000 gold and silver coins which confirm a burial after AD 407/8, plus 100 spoons and some beautiful jewellery including a bracelet 'to Lady Juliana' and an unusual body brooch. Here you will see a set of ten silver ladles *(PRBP.1994.4–8.42–61)* with the chi-rho just below the bowl of each. Above them are spoons, many of which have the chi-rho and alpha and omega engraved in the bowl.

On the right of *case 18* displays replicas of the **Canterbury Hoard** discovered in 1962. Notice the replicas of spoons and toothpick with Christian symbols (PRB 1962.11–8.1–19). In this case also is an oval **pewter dish** *(PRB 1897.12–18.32)* discovered in Appleshaw, Hampshire with a fish symbol in the centre.

Close by is another replica of a large **silver tray** *(PRB P.1992.6–1.1)*. On the underside is the chi rho emblem, and the tray has an inscription that reveals it was a present given by Bishop Exuperius (bishop of Toulouse who died sometime after AD 410). This was discovered in 1729 at Risley Park in Derbyshire which makes it the first Roman silver utensil recorded as found in Britain; sadly those who found it did not realise its importance because they broke up their

Above: Water Newton silverware from the 4th century, used in Christian worship (PRB p.1975.10-2.5)

treasure and left only a drawing, from which this electrostatic replica has been made.

On the other side of this case notice a **pewter dish** *(PRB 1927.1–6.1)* with crude crosses inscribed in the centre, and a **spoon** *(PRB P.1971.5–1.1)*.

In *case 17* you will find the **Water Newton Treasure** also displaying the chi-rho symbol and an intriguing inscription.

Discovered in 1975 at Water Newton near Peterborough in Cambridgeshire (Peterborough was the Roman town of Durobrivae), they were clearly all intended for Christian ceremonies. Although they were badly damaged, they are the

earliest Christian silverware from the Roman Empire. The large dish *(PRBP.1975.10–2.7)* reveals the outline of the chi-rho which has been marked out presumably to be engraved later. Some of these items were dedicated by Publianus whose name is engraved round the larger bowl *(PRBP.1975.10-2.5)*. It includes also the words *sanctum altare tuum domine subnixus honoro*. The true significance of the final two words is somewhat obscure but one translation of this inscription is: 'your holy altar, Lord, I am trusting, I honour'—it is uncertain whether the trust and honour is in the Lord *(domine)* or the altar. It also includes two chi-rho monograms. Other items were dedicated by three women: Amcilla, Innocentia and Viventia—perhaps members of the same congregation.

Personal Jewellery

In *case 11* against the left hand wall half way down the room in the second panel from the right *no. 34* you will find a **silver fibula** or clasp *(PRB 1954.12–6.1)* and on the next panel nos 28 and 29 **two gold rings** *(PRB P1983 10–3.1 and 1984 10–1.1)* each with the chi-rho symbol on them. These are all items dated from the 4th century.

Cash and pewter

In *case 10* (behind you) is a poor quality bronze coin from the time of *Emperor Magnentius* dated AD 353. On the obverse is the Emperor and on the reverse is the

chi-rho between the alpha and omega. We have seen a better example of this in Room 68 case 5 panel 4 *no*. 13 page 106.

Above: A beautiful fourth century gold ring with the chi rho emblem reversed for the purpose of sealing (PRB P1983 10–3.1)

Top: The chi-rho emblem on a coin of Magnentius from room 68 page 107

Above: Fourth century Roman wall decoration from Lullingstone in Kent with the Christian chi rho and alpha and omega (PRB 1967 4–7.1)

Case 9 displays a *pewter ingot* (PRB 1891 2–17.1) of the 4th century. This was dredged from the Thames and the merchant's marks on it include Christian symbols.

In *case 14* there are bronze statues of the Emperors Claudius (PRB 1965 12–1.1)–see Acts 11:28; 18:2–and Nero (PRB 1813.2–13.1) under whom Paul and Peter were martyred.

In the centre of this room (*cases 8 and 6*) is a display of Roman military equipment found in England, and a model of Housesteads fort on Hadrian's Wall. See case 2.

Finally—home decorating

At the far end of this room you will find a *mosaic from Hinton St Mary,* Dorset. This is a temporary display. In 1963 a blacksmith was digging new foundations for his smithy when he stumbled across the remains of what proved to be a large Roman building complex including a villa. Dated some time in the fourth century, this is one of the earliest known representations of Christ and the only mosaic of Christ found in Roman Europe; you will see the chi-rho motif behind the head of Christ. Around the edge are what may be the four evangelists. See page 108.

Return up this room and go towards the right-hand corner by the door you entered.

Here is the *Lullingstone wall decoration* (PRB 1967 4–7.1) from a Roman villa in Kent. The room in which these were found was used for Christian worship. It was excavated in 1949. The villa was built late in the first century but subsequently altered and pagan worship is evident. By the 4th century the owners had adopted Christianity and hence the chi-rho motif and the frieze of Christians at prayer (the large panel above). To the left of the frieze is a mosaic of the chi-rho with alpha and omega. This was probably a house church, or private chapel—only a few examples of house churches are known in the entire Roman Empire.

There is no certain evidence of Christian emblems found in Britain before the fourth century—yet!

When did merchants, soldiers and civil servants first bring the gospel to England? Hopefully the answers to this and many more questions may soon be revealed in a field or on a building site by an archaeologist or by some unsuspecting worker!

Your shortest route to the entrance hall from here is to leave this **Room 49 into Room 41** and turn right (past the marble sarcophagus) into **Rooms 40 and 36.** Here you will find lifts to your right or straight ahead, the main Victorian staircase—which has been used by generations of visitors for over 150 years.

Top: The centre of the Hinton St Mary mosaic
Above: The main entrance hall from the Victorian staircase

A glossary of archaeological words that are either used in this book or will be found in your tour of the Museum

Cartouche	An oval ring enclosing the hieroglyphs of the name or title of an Egyptian king.
Cuneiform	The wedge-shaped signs of Babylonians and Assyrian writing. See page 28
Cylinder	A memorial or record inscribed with cuneiform script onto clay (less often stone) in a barrel-shape.
Cylinder seal	The typical stone seal used in Babylonia and Assyria; up to 5 cms (2 inches) in height with a design engraved around the circumference.
Cursive	Letters of the alphabet that were joined together in writing. In Greek this joining took place around the 7th century AD.
Demotic script	The cursive form of Egyptian hieroglyphs used for ordinary documents in Egypt from around 650BC to AD 500. The word means 'of the people' and refers to writing that was used for everyday documents.
Dyad	A pair of statues often carved from the same block.
Dynasty	A line of rulers generally from the same family.
Fertile Crescent	The territory stretching from Egypt in the south through Palestine, Syria and Mesopotamia down to the Persian Gulf. It forms a large crescent shape of the most fertile land. See map on page 26.
Hieratic script	A shortened form of Egyptian hieroglyphs for writing on papyrus.
Hieroglyphic	The earliest writing from Egypt and elsewhere that represents a word, syllable or sound in the form of pictures. From the Greek meaning 'a sacred carving'. See page 27.
Ingot	A length of cast metal, usually gold or silver but also lead or iron.
Lapis lazuli	The mineral sodium aluminium silicate and sulphur in the form of a bright blue gemstone stone that was commonly used for jewellery. It was mined in Afghanistan.
Levant	The lands to the east of the Mediterranean where the sun rises; from French lever—to rise.
Minuscule (var. miniscule)	Lower case letters that were later joined up into cursive writing in the 7th century. The opposite of uncial.
MS	The short form of 'manuscript', a handwritten document—the plural is MSS; lit. 'written by hand'.
Mummy	From Arabic mummia meaning bitumen or rock-like as mummies ended up being black and hard.
Obelisk	A four-sided, stone pillar tapering at the top; usually inscribed with texts as a monument or record. See page 82.

Obverse	The side of a coin with the main image on it. The other side is the reverse.
Ostraca	Pieces of broken pottery on which messages were written. Singular—ostracon. See page 42.
Ossuary	Small box in which human bones were placed.
Pewter	A combination of tin and lead.
Pharaoh	The title of the kings of Egypt from around 14th century BC. The word comes from the Egyptian *per-aa* meaning 'great house'.
Porphyry	A hard rock, largely composed of crystals, quarried in ancient Egypt.
Potsherd	A piece of broken pottery or glass. See also Shard.
Prism	A hollow or solid object with several parallel sides. See page 48.
Pyramids	In Egypt, gigantic tombs: the shape may represent a theory of creation.
Relief	A piece of sculpture in which the objects stand out from the background. See page 87.
Reverse	The side of the coin which has the secondary image on it. The principal side is known as the obverse.
Sarcophagus	A stone coffin often sculptured or inscribed. It comes from a Greek word meaning 'flesh-eating'.
Scarab	The dung beetle (scarabaeus sacer) regarded as sacred by the ancient Egyptians; it is often found in the form of amulets, ornaments etc. See page 45
Seal	The impression made on clay or wax by a stone seal or signet to mark ownership; it is also used of the tool that makes the impression. In Babylonia these were generally cylindrical, in Egypt the scarab was used, and in the Levant more commonly a stamp. See page 35.
Shard	See Potsherd. A variant of 'sherd' a short form of potsherd.
Stela	An upright pillar with an inscription and sometimes a sculpture.
Tell	The Semitic word for a ruin-mound that is made up from the successive layers of occupancy of a site. See page 19.
Uncial	The early form of modern capital letters; the uncials, which are un-joined letters, are found in Greek manuscripts up to the 8th century BC.
Votive offering	An offering made to the gods in fulfilment of a vow.
Ziggurat	A series of platforms each on top of and smaller than the previous one with a shrine on top and steps leading up to it. The usual form of the main temple in Mesopotamian cities. See page 26.

AUTHORS

Brian Edwards is the author of twelve books including two historical biographies, one of which was used as the basis for a British Channel Four television film on William Tyndale. He is an international speaker, a member of the Tyndale Society and the editor of this Travel Guide series. Brian, whose wife died in 1998, lives in Surrey and is the father of two sons and has three granddaughters.

Clive Anderson is a member of The British Museum Society, The British School of Archaeology in Iraq, and the Egypt Exploration Society; he leads tours to the Middle East and Egypt and is the author of *Travel with Spurgeon* in this series. Clive lives in Hampshire and is married to Amanda; they have one son.

ACKNOWLEDGMENTS

The authors would like to express their appreciation to the many people who have assisted in the preparation of this guide: in particular Professors Donald Wiseman and Alan Millard, and Mr Terence Mitchell, for their invaluable help, encouragement and advice. We are grateful also to Paul Gardner, Photography and Imaging Manager at The British Museum, for his helpful cooperation.

For serious research as well as group outings

This series is unique: each book combines biography with travel guide. Notes, maps and photographs help you to explore Britain's distinctive heritage. The first three in this series introduce John Bunyan, author of *Pilgrim's Progress;* Charles Haddon Spurgeon, 'Prince of Preachers', and William Booth, founder of The Salvation Army.

For personal study at home

For individuals on the trail

128 PAGES   **£9.99 EACH**

★ PLACES OF INTEREST TO VISIT

★ PACKED WITH COLOUR PHOTOS

★ CLEAR ILLUSTRATED MAPS

★ GREAT GIFT IDEA

★ CALL DAY ONE PUBLICATIONS ON ☎ 01568 613 740

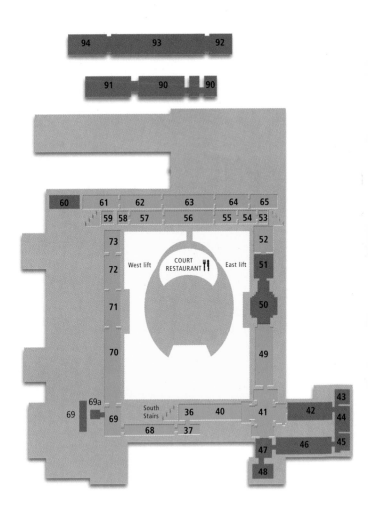

Upper floor Rooms 36–73, 90–94

KEY ■ Rooms you will either visit or walk through in this guide
■ Rooms you will not need to enter in this guide